PRAISE FOR
The (Real) Revolution in Military Affairs

"Martyanov's book is, in a way, two books. One is about the revolution in military affairs that has left the United States behind. The other is about the self-medicating and propagandistic version of reality that Americans mistake for reality. Martyanov convinced me that the Pentagon's war planners need to upgrade their understanding of war and how to conduct one, but I found more interesting the fake reality supported by controlled explanations from which Americans seem unable to escape that is described in the other part of his book. It turns out that it is not only the insouciant general population but also the ruling elites themselves who are locked in The Matrix."

—PAUL CRAIG ROBERTS

"…Martyanov sees the world at the beginning of a new era in which global power will be rearranged towards a multi-polar system. The foundation for that is the real revolution in military affairs that Russia and others created while the U.S. was still busy with telling itself that its power will only ever increase.

"In his postscriptum Maryanov states that the U.S. is in reality a power in decline.

"Andrei Martyanov's book provides indispensable knowledge for anyone who wants to understand the current geo-political developments."

—MOON OF ALABAMA

The (Real) Revolution in Military Affairs

ANDREI MARTYANOV

Clarity Press, Inc.

© 2019 ANDREI MARTYANOV
ISBN: 978-1-949762-07-5
EBOOK: 978-1-949762-08-2

In-house editor: Diana G. Collier
Cover: R. Jordan P. Santos

Library of Congress Control Number:2019942048

Clarity Press, Inc.
2625 Piedmont Rd. NE, Suite 56
Atlanta, GA. 30324
http://www.claritypress.com

TABLE OF CONTENTS

PREFACE

Just recently a respectable, conservative, and to their greatest credit, anti-war publication, *The American Conservative*, unleashed a scathing, well-justified, criticism on warmongers and Iran hawks such as David Brooks and Bret Stephens, who write primarily for the *New York Times*. Both Brooks and Stephens, among very many similar others, fancy themselves pundits, analysts, columnists and commentators with a focus on geopolitics and international relations. No doubt, they analyze and comment on those issues and, as is the case with any humanities-educated pundits among leading American mainstream media personalities, they boast an impressive (for media figures) set of credentials in all kinds of disciplines related to media—from history, to political philosophy to journalism. What neither Brooks nor Stephens, as well as the vast majority of American political class, have as credentials is even an infinitesimally small background in the subjects on which all of them are trying to comment, analyze and (for those in position of political power) even make decisions—warfare.

Warfare is a geopolitical tool of the first order. In fact, geopolitics as a field of interaction of nations cannot exist without it. Warfare, in the end, formed and continues to be anchored in the human condition, and as a result, in our political, social, economic and cultural institutions. No understanding of warfare is possible without understanding its most important tools, weapons and people, tactics and operational art. It is precisely the field in which American political class has zero competencies—they simply do not teach nor grant degrees in what amounts to military science in the United States. Obviously, rubbing shoulders with American military top brass and listening to rumors may create among some pundits and political figures an illusion that they know how the military operates or how wars are fought—but it is only an illusion. Truth to be told, regurgitation of the few, beaten to death, political talking points in the media sphere doesn't require any serious background in anything of substance. On the other hand— writing a graduate thesis on Anti-Submarine Warfare operations in Arctic or on Fractionate Exchange Rates during air operations in the EW-dense environment—are the skills of a completely different level and backgrounds of which modern American pundits and an army of armchair "military analysts" cannot conceive. But precisely these skills and knowledge are the key to not only understanding of a modern warfare but to grasping geopolitical reality which is increasingly complex and rests on the foundation of the ever-evolving and revolutionary military technologies.

To forestall possible accusations of disparagement of the field of humanities leveled against me, it should be noted that my point is completely different here: modern war between nation-states became so complex, in reflection of the tools of such wars, that it is an axiom, not even a theorem, that people who cannot grasp fundamental mathematical, physical, tactical and operational principles on which modern weapon systems operate are simply not qualified in the minimal degree to offer their opinions on the issues of warfare, intelligence operations and military technology without appropriate backgrounds. Failing that, what can one think but that they are merely in the business of content provision (filling space/entertainment) or of propagating the official line— of propaganda, in short—mostly with regard to warmongering? In today's information-oversaturated world of massive egos nurtured by the dopamine of public visibility and of American politics turned into showbiz, these are the types who dominate the discussion on the most important, vital issue of war and peace in our time. And, truth to be told, the Theory of Operations or Operational Planning are on an order of magnitude harder to learn than, say, Comparative Politics in the course of Political Science, even though this Politics of necessity is still revolving around economic and military power.

I am completely aware how difficult it is today for any person, bombarded by salvo upon salvo of irrelevant, misleading, useless information, to try to get a handle on the historic change unfolding before their very eyes. It is impossible to get a handle on this without understanding how politics is defined by elements of power, among which real economic and military factors are the main drivers of this change. In this book I am trying to give at least some, by far not all, of the ABCs in military affairs and explain how a revolution in military affairs, a real one, many times declared prematurely, now shapes our modern world and how modern weaponry completely and dramatically, indeed in a revolutionary way, has changed the global balance of power, despite many models predicting very different and much less dramatic scenarios.

I tried my best, at the insistence of my wonderful publisher, to stay away from math or to simplify it. You, the reader, will be the one who will pass judgement on my success, or otherwise, in trying to avoid getting into the calculus or probabilities. While some high school basic math, including some basic factoring, will still be needed for its greatest appreciation, this book was written in a such a way that those who do not want to deal with any math at all can simply skip any parts with mathematics in them; this will not distort the main message of the book.

I can only hope that the knowledge readers will gain through this book will help to increase public awareness of the deadly consequences of even a conventional war between global superpowers and will help to dispel the war propaganda being pushed on the public by ignorant and incompetent pundits who have no business offering even an iota of their opinions on what is today a Revolution in Military Affairs of historic magnitude.

3

The Absence of War: An Omission in the Western Definition of "a Good Life"

In *The Great Delusion,* his latest work on the fallacy of a liberal view of the world which has been enthusiastically embraced in the United States, John Mearsheimer elaborates extensively on his opinion of the objective of the political ideologies and views of our time—a good life.[1] Following a liberal, by definition relativist, view of the world, Mearsheimer concludes, leads to truth becoming very elusive—and accordingly, so does a universal definition of a good life. The title of his latest treatise is a good indicator that Mearsheimer, one of the few leading mainstream American political scientists, along with thinkers of scale, such as Paul Craig Roberts, recognizes the economic and intellectual crisis of liberalism as well as liberalism's utter failure to provide any coherent answer as to what a good life, indeed, is. But Mearsheimer doesn't go far enough. Unlike Paul Craig Roberts, Mearsheimer limits his critique of liberalism to what he defines broadly as nationalism, failing to address the main economic drivers impelling liberal aggression, and continuing to take the United States at face value as a liberal democracy. The United States is no longer a liberal democracy, if ever it was one.

Rather than trying to formulate precisely what "the good life" really is, an impossible task in a world of a vast number of cultures, circumstances and outlooks, we should abandon the self-centered ruminations which persist in Western political science, and recognize that, in universal terms, the most important part of the *good life* expression is *life* itself, first and foremost, with it then being *good* being predicated on a number of extremely complex causative factors. Very many of those factors are often viewed in a pro-forma fashion by American political science due to the fact that most of those scientists have undergone none of the crucial experiences that much of humankind outside the borders of the United States, endure daily and have done for centuries—the struggle for mere survival. That is to say, large numbers of people, even whole nations, fight for *life itself,* viewing this life being *good* as an important but at best a secondary consideration.

Discounting natural conditions and disasters such as earthquakes or epidemics as reasons for the fight for survival, the sad reality is that all other factors which make people fight for life are anything but natural—all of them have human causation, be it the sanctions applied on 20th century Iraq that led to the deaths of hundreds of thousands of children, or the misnamed R2P destruction of relatively stable and prosperous Libya in 2011. Conflict is a part of human nature, with war being the apogee of conflict, which then becomes armed, and really has defined human life since the dawn of civilization. Humans become violent under some conditions and this leads to a fight for life by those who are weaker against the violence applied by those stronger. The American political science class has spent and continues to spend significant time and resources allegedly studying the nature of conflict, that is to say the nature of war, but bar some very few exceptions, remains remarkably ignorant on the extreme nature of that conflict—that it involves life and death for large numbers of persons under usually horrific circumstances whose impact then shapes both societies, the victor as well as the loser. As Daniel Larison of *The American Conservative* noted in his piece with the symptomatic title, "Why the U.S. Fails to Understand its Adversaries":

Unfortunately, the U.S. is remarkably bad at understanding these things accurately. This is not just a Trump administration failing. Most American politicians and policymakers routinely misjudge the intentions and goals of our adversaries, and they often invent a fantasy version of the regime in question that leads them astray again and again. One reason for this is that it is simply easier to project our assumptions about what a regime must want than it is to make the effort to see things as they do. Another reason is that many of our politicians and policymakers mistakenly think that if they try to understand an adversary's views that must somehow mean that they sympathize with the adversary or condone its behavior. Instead of trying to know their enemy, our leaders would prefer not to for fear of being "tainted" by the experience. This lack of knowledge is compounded in some cases by the absence of normal diplomatic relations with the adversary. Our leaders are encouraged to take this self-defeating approach to international problems by a political culture that rewards the people that strike tough-sounding-but-ignorant poses about a problem and marginalizes those that seek to understand it as fully as possible.[2]

Larison is one of very few American scholars who admits such a disturbing fact, but the problem lies even deeper— American scholarship in general, and especially the field of so-called political science, fails, due to America's lucky geographic insulation from the horrors of continental war, to grasp the nature and applications of what is the foundation of the fight for survival and, allegedly, the fight for a *good life*—military power. This failure was inevitable in a society which has, when compared to many other societies, a rather limited experience with fighting for its own survival, despite the incessant government fearmongering about foreign threats—which until 9/11 were largely unrealized. And even then, despite being spectacular in the worst meaning of the word, terrorist acts of 9/11 were in no way realistically threatening the existence of United States as a nation and of her political institutions. In other words—America's survival was not in question.

Liberalism, in its different contemporary manifestations, such as globalist capitalism, also known as globalization, has a "stellar" record of using threats as a primary tool in international relations. Globalism is aggressive for a number of reasons ranging from purely economic interests to convictions of cultural superiority. These form a ballast for what goes on to become military aggression, easily resorted to because of the often complete inability to understand the practice (what really happens during warfare) and the consequences of the application of military power (what really happens as a result of that trauma and destruction) and accordingly an appreciation of how to achieve a global military balance precluding war. This is not to say that liberal academe doesn't try to understand this—it tries repeatedly, including by creating a variety of models and theories of international relations and of wars, but too many of those theories are nothing more than whiteboard abstracts. It warrants noting that for all its aggressiveness in the post–WW II period, globalism's main driver, the United States, produced a rather mediocre record of military accomplishments, while providing a cornucopia of theories on how to win wars and what is military balance. Many theories have come and gone trying to explain how war and international relations interact, be that Stephen Biddle's "New System," or Foreign Policy Realism in its mind-boggling variety from Structural to Offensive to Defensive theories, or even Offense-Defense Theory, such as being defined, among many others, by Charles Glaser and Chaim Kaufman, as a cost-ratio of offense to defense.[3]

Few of those, however, answer the question as to what military power and balance really are, what is their nature and what is their role in the fight for survival. That brings forth a hugely important moral issue of who is the victim and who is the predator in a dyadic relation of nations. Without addressing this question, no amount of Offense-Defense or any other reasoning will help in understanding the process of the formation of military power and balance in the modern world. In other words, it matters a great deal *why* a nation builds its own military power and what it intends to use it for. The answer defines a key condition for a good life for the potential victim—survival, preservation of life, that is, or in other words an ability to live in peace thanks to the strength of arms. There is no good life without peace, and liberalism is not capable of defining that as a key component of a good life, due to liberalism and its scholarship living in a complete delusion about the predatory intentions driving its own economic and military (often grossly exaggerated) capability.

War is a mere continuation of policy by other means. This dictum by Carl Von Clausewitz is known today by most humans with even a basic college education, the same as one-liners by Nietzsche or Sun Tzu. What is not known to many, though, is that even within the last 30 years those Clausewitzian "means" of war have changed so dramatically that the foundational nature of military power and military balance has simply escaped philosophical and political scientists' grip and requires a set of skills, knowledge and competencies which are not to be found in the very fields which proclaim otherwise. After more than 24 years of what is tantamount to liberalism's warfare all over the globe, the grasp of the West in general, and that of Americans in particular, of the foundational reasons for their pursuit and acquisition of military power—predation—remains elusive. Even taking into account the agenda-pushing raison d'être of very many of the contemporary U.S. think tanks working in the field of war, the extent of ignorance of the foundational intent of warfare, as opposed to how it is conducted, is simply startling, manifesting itself in downright delusional war concepts or narratives which continue to obfuscate the American view of military power which knows no other posture but an aggressive one. Even John Mearsheimer, who has a reputation as a foreign policy realist, and who is ready to criticize liberalism, accords positive power to liberalism, supporting Fukuyama's dubious statement of liberalism defeating fascism.[4] All this despite massive empirical evidence to the contrary—the extremely well documented contributions and costs of defeating fascism in WW II which refute such a claim, indicating almost 80% of the forces of Nazi Germany were destroyed at the radically non-liberal Eastern Front. This is surprising evidence of a blind spot by people who claim to be academics and knowledgeable. But that is the problem with Western political science or, more generally, the humanities field—a stubborn lack of desire to operate with facts.

It was Socrates, via Plato's *Republic,* who came up with the prescription which would, in his mind, make life better for all:

Until, then, kings are philosophers, or philosophers are kings, cities will never cease from ill: no, nor the human race; nor will our ideal polity ever come into being.[5]

Socrates' idea, formed in the times of sail and wars fought with swords, shields and spears, seemed reasonable since philosophers and intellectuals of the era had little problem grasping the essence of warfare, the marketplace and industry as it existed 2,400 years back. Any inquisitive mind then could learn a great deal about different manifestations of human activity given that it was greatly limited by the primitive conditions of the time. Philosophers could build and lead armies then, they also could be kings or Caesars, such as Marcus Aurelius who definitely satisfied Socrates' desire to see a philosopher as a king and vice-versa. Today things have changed dramatically—the modern world is filled with philosophers and their other contemporary iterations such as political scientists, sociologists or even economists, yet their grasp of the modern world is growing weaker and very few of them are capable to grasp all the complexity of the ongoing processes of this increasingly puzzling modern humanity.

In fact, increasingly what used to be philosophy's prerogative—finding the answers to life's most complex questions by reasoning on the basis of abstractions and principles—cannot be done anymore. It was possible to assert this prerogative in the times of sword and sail, but in the times of space travel, neural networks, instant propagation of information and robots, something else entirely is needed and mere appeal to well-learned philosophical wisdom is not enough.

Reasoning can no longer be based on broad generalizations only. In fact, uninformed reasoning can, and often does, lead to unexpected and not always benign results. In the modern world saturated, if not altogether overwhelmed with data, one has to have at least some rudimentary tools which allow one to filter, systematize and analyze this data. Philosophy and political science simply do not provide viable tools for that—the reason being rather simple: most modern philosophers, political scientists and other representatives

10

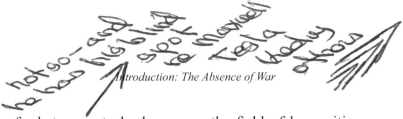

of what came to be known as the field of humanities are not educated in the field of modern technology. It is not, then, surprising that many people highly educated in precise sciences such as the late Stephen Hawking, Carl Sagan or quantum physicists such as Dr. Michio Kaku, have made and continue to make massive contributions to modern philosophy. After all, Rene Descartes was one of the greatest mathematical minds in history, while being one of history's the greatest philosophers.

There is a simple explanation to it. Those holding a modern Ph.D. in philosophy or political science, unless they have a serious education and experience in other fields, will be hard-pressed to derive any sensible conclusions on automation, for example, barring some self-evident and easily accessible truths such as that increased automation removes workers from the manufacturing floor, thus increasing unemployment. This same Ph.D. will have very little knowledge of what goes into the fundamental technological principles relating to the automation of modern industry or, for that matter, how G-code interpreters work for Computer Numerical Control machining centers and what is required to run them—a knowledge domain belonging to college-educated engineers.

Modern warfare therefore becomes an unfathomable conundrum for the modern humanities-educated American intellectual elites who nonetheless dominate the top echelons of power and a vast network of think tanks, as confirmed by the appalling record of failure of most contemporary American military-strategic assessments of America's foes and of the short and long term technological trends in war.

This is not to mention a dangerous misjudgment of America's own capabilities. Needless to say, many so-called "strategies" and concepts—some of them disastrous for both the United States and the nations it feels it can and must destroy—are also often advanced by people proficient in ancient history, philosophy, political science and even the theory of international relations, with some game theory attached to it, but seldom by people who are true military professionals capable of counteracting politically motivated and overly-rationalized aggressive ideas by serious military (operational and technological, that is) knowledge and experience as was the case with Admiral Fallon in 2008.

Fallon had enough fortitude and professional and human integrity to sacrifice his career by openly challenging the neo-conservative-dominated George W. Bush Administration's mad plans for waging war on Iran.[6] This obviously took more than just a sober, competent assessment by a military professional; it took human qualities of the highest order to prevent what could have been a geopolitical disaster on a massive scale. Needless to say, the war plans against Iran were reasoned and rationalized by people such as Donald Rumsfeld, Richard Perle and Paul Wolfowitz, none of whom had spent a day serving in cadre officer uniform, nor had any serious technology-oriented background, with Wolfowitz getting his B.A. in mathematics before continuing to his degree in political science.

This is precisely the environment and the level of expertise, or lack thereof, which is largely responsible for formulating U.S. aggressive policies based on the delusion or myth of American military-technological superiority over its foes—against whom it still cannot win a single war. Political scientists do not make good strategists, they simply lack an understanding of the key, and very complex, issues which form geopolitical and military-strategic reality because most of them have neither the military-academic or the precise sciences backgrounds crucial for developing appropriate tools for sound analyses and forecasts of global geopolitical and military trends. Putting it in laymen's lingo, one has to know how things work. Those educated in the modern American political science and philosophy field don't. They don't because modern military technology became very complex as did the tactical, operational and strategic aspects of its use.

Studying and memorizing endless taxonomies constituting the catalog of knowledge of political science is not the same as studying physical principles realized in modern weapons systems and the platforms carrying them, or what goes into operational research and the planning of operations—those are very different tasks in their level of complexity. In such a case, it is not surprising that the mythology of American technological and military exceptionalism became a driving force behind what my earlier work, *Losing Military Supremacy: The Myopia of American Strategic Planning,* identified as a dangerous lacuna in American strategic planning.

It would also make it counterintuitive to view offensive military power as anything even remotely related to the "good" life, or for that matter, any life at all. Which is how this power is widely perceived around the globe once one leaves the rigid constraints of liberalism's narratives and begins to view the world for what it is, not how it is construed primarily by the Western media, think tanks and the political science class.

This book, while deconstructing the liberal narrative, tries to reconstruct some important technological, tactical, operational and strategic aspects of military power and how it relates to the necessary formation of a global military balance, and in the end, to the survival of the human civilization.

CHAPTER 1

The "Thucydides Trap" Delusion: The Incoherence and Fallacy of Contemporary Geopolitical Concepts

In March 2018 an influential American magazine, *The Diplomat,* published a short piece by Francis P. Sempa on the Thucydides Trap. In this piece Sempa, citing a collection of articles and essays by U.S. senior military officers titled *Avoiding the Trap: U.S. Strategy and Policy for Competing in the Asia-Pacific Beyond the Rebalance,* noted in amusement that:

> The most remarkable aspect of this study is the lack of "hawkishness" among the contributors, most of whom are high-level military officers. Only one article asserts that China intends to become the Asia-Pacific's regional hegemon and is following a step-by-step expansionist strategy to displace the United States in the region. Two of the contributors emphasize the need to strengthen and improve U.S. defense ties to Japan and India in order to counterbalance China's military growth.[1]

It is, sadly, not surprising that Sempa, an attorney by education and a political "scientist" by occupation,[2] is surprised by the fact of military professionals being reluctant to take political science whiteboard theories to heart. But military professionals are absolutely correct in their reluctance and they have ample reasons to be suspicious of international relations concepts cooked up in the deep recesses of Western in general, and American in particular, political science kitchens populated by people who, for the most part, have zero military backgrounds and experiences.

But what is this Thucydides Trap? The term was coined by the American political scientist Graham Allison and is a so-called geopolitical model based on ancient Greek historian Thucydides' conclusion that "The growth of the power of Athens, and the alarm which this inspired in Lacedaemon, made war inevitable."[3]

Here, the obsession of the contemporary American political science class with the Peloponnesian War, an ancient historical event at the foundation of neoconservatives-inspired American foreign policy and the resultant military disasters of the 21st century, manifests itself yet again. In Allison's view the dynamics of the evolution of the power balance between the United States and China can easily be viewed in parallel to relations between Athens and Sparta which led to the Peloponnesian War more than 2400 years ago. It is difficult to completely rationalize American elites' obsession with that war but comparing China to Athens and the United States to Sparta is not only ahistorical, it is simply meaningless. There is very little doubt that American political and military elites are concerned with the growth of China's economic, political and military power. This is understandable. But the so-called *Trap* which makes—in theory—the war between China and the United States almost inevitable is for the most part a figment of imagination of people who have, at best, a very vague understanding of real warfare of the 21st century. This ignorance is a defining feature of the American political class.

China's Xi was explicit when stating, correctly, that the Thucydides Trap simply doesn't exist.[4] Moreover, the whole concept of this trap didn't sit well even with some of Russia's

[handwritten margin note at top: Real American Resurrection, Healing and transformation into a soul and a soul of noble humble wise warriors —]

[handwritten margin notes in right margin: Justice, war is against NATO forces ... of limited reasoning]

most radical pro-Western liberals known for their blind, uncritical following of most American geopolitical and ideological concepts. As one of them stated, the Thucydides Trap is a *Political Scientist's Trap.*[5] Of course, war between China and the United States may still happen, but as even the summary to the Study which so surprised Francis Sempa with its "lack of hawkishness" states:

> Long-range success in the Asia-Pacific region will only come from effective international cooperation. This cooperation must include China. In keeping with the 2015 U.S. National Security Strategy, we confirm the U.S. position to "welcome the rise of a stable, peaceful, and prosperous China." To that end, the overarching strategic task for the United States is how to accommodate China's rise. America must not constrain the responsible rise of China in the region and globally, but at the same time should provide a check on Chinese power by protecting U.S. and partner national interests. This check will come through the effective use of a rules-based international order, but ultimately it will be empowered by a position of U.S. strength across the elements of national power.[6]

The elements of national power is what really matters in this statement and it requires a serious review of such elements in order to understand that war with China, whose power undeniably continues to grow, can only happen within the conventional paradigm. Otherwise, with the war going nuclear, none of the objectives by either side will be attained and the possibility of global thermonuclear conflict will arise. A nuclear argument is what really makes all talk about the Thucydides Trap a foolhardy business, because Mutually Assured Destruction (MAD) is the factor which makes any parallels to ancient warfare history irrelevant. It is not the only factor, but it is surely the most important one.

A possible nuclear scenario between the United States and China does not require any serious elaboration since even laymen have enough understanding of the catastrophic global consequences of two (or more) nuclear superpowers engaging in nuclear exchange. It is a scenario which must be avoided by all means and it seems those who in the United States understand that best of all are American military professionals. The same applies to the Chinese military. But while there are a few more-or-less competent and influential people who speak about the fallacy of Allison's *Trap,* one has to point out a simple fact that the Thucydides Trap of sorts has been known to mankind since the very dawn of human civilization. Way before Ancient Greece, it was observed in the animal world, when aging leaders of a herd are challenged by younger and more ambitious competitors. It was and is also observed in the world of individual humans all the time— consider sports, whose very premise is built on challenging the status quo, be that boxing, track and field or soccer. In general, Allison's Thucydides Trap is known to humanity as a competition and not all competitions end up in wars. Even in animal kingdom the winner of a leadership role in herd doesn't kill its competitor in very many cases. This is not to mention the fact that Athens, Sparta and Thucydides himself did not operate in the context of nuclear weapons, net-centric warfare, stand-off high-precision weapons and combined arms operations, which even in purely conventional form can paralyze and defeat a modern nation-state, or cause human losses on an unimaginable scale. These factors must change any kind of generalizations related to military and war based on ancient history.

This brings us to the more important issue—historical parallels. Drawing historical parallels is an extremely dangerous business wrought with huge risks of miscalculation and learning wrong lessons. History, certainly, does provide some valuable lessons but at this stage the entirety of the term *history,* as it was understood even fairly recently, does not reflect the immense complexity of human development and activity for the last roughly hundred years. Those developments can no longer be described within traditional frameworks because an greater number causalities are being afflicted not just due to human nature but now to the technology created by and in service to it. As technology becomes increasingly complex its ramifications become beyond the grasp of many humanities-educated historians who lack the cognitive apparatus for understanding and describing technology and its effect on the events. Modern war is highly technological. What used to be a few tactical and operational factors to be considered by military leaders such as Napoleon, Kutuzov or Grant, today becomes a vast and complex set of variables needed to be considered by leaders while making a decision. There is a reason why contemporary military leaders have very strong backgrounds in fundamental sciences and many of them have serious engineering backgrounds in addition to rigorous training in tactics, operational art and strategy. Complexity and the huge number of factors influencing modern warfare are behind increasing automation (computerization) of the environment in which decisions are being made by commanders.

While general principles of warfare and what is called strategy has, since the times of Clausewitz, remained largely static and generally similar for many modern armies, the approach to the application of those principles has grown in complexity exponentially.[7] In times of muskets and linear tactics, an officer commanding a company or battalion would have had little trouble understanding a general plan on the battle or even the campaign. Today, such understanding requires long years of highly specialized education and very serious background in military technology. Without this background there can be no serious understanding of modern warfare—this is simply a hard fact of life. This is where drawing historical parallels becomes a very dangerous business. Even many non-military people understand this danger and, in fact, some have even reflected this danger in modern film.

A 1980 sci-fi Hollywood flick, *The Final Countdown,* starring Kirk Douglas and Martin Sheen, is an excellent example of such an awareness. While the movie deals with a possible time paradox when the nuclear powered aircraft carrier *USS Nimitz* is transported, due to a freaky storm, from 1980 to December 7, 1941, a few hours before the Japanese aviation attack on Pearl-Harbor, the historic ramifications of such an event become clear immediately. Even the most unsophisticated observer could easily foresee, even without understanding basic technological principles, that a single U.S. Navy nuclear aircraft carrier and its air wing which included F-14 Tomcat fighters would have very little difficulty destroying 360 Japanese piston aircraft due to the modern American carrier's advanced electronic sensors and the overwhelming advantage modern jet aircraft had over 1930s-designed combat planes in speed, maneuverability and weapons. It came down to a complete tactical, operational and technological mismatch, even if portrayed in a fictional setting.

Thus the irresistible question arises—what lessons could have been drawn from Japanese actions on December 7, 1941 in tactical and operational senses to be applied to modern times? Of course, the lesson of a strategic and operational surprise is valid, but this lesson is as old as the Trojan horse concept. The truth is, few of those lessons, other than the ever present and generally understood necessity to develop better weapons and sensors, could have been drawn. And here is the point—technology became a main, albeit not the only, driver behind tactical and operational requirements. Of course issues of morale, culture, and the financial, economic and social (but not yet digital) dimensions of war and, in the end, leadership never lost their significance but it goes without saying that in the fight between even the squadron of *Mitsubishi A6M Zero* and a pair of *Grumman F-14 Tomcat* jet aircraft, chances of the WW II piston airplanes surviving such an encounter approach zero—due primarily for a gigantic technological mismatch, even if one assumes that the pilots of the *Zeros* are the best fighter pilots of their time. Only by answering the question *why* things work one way and not the other can one begin to see why falling back on history, granted it is based on facts, not fantasies, is never a good idea, especially when trying to promote rather broad and shaky concepts such as Thucydides Trap.

Applying lessons from the Falklands War, from the Battle of Lepanto, or even from the chronologically much closer Battle of Midway, for 21st Century naval warfare requires a lot of operational and historical finesse if one wants to avoid being contrived in a manner such as, say, applying lessons of 19th century cavalry to modern armored warfare. Russia's Chief of General Staff Valery Gerasimov was explicit: "Each war represents an isolated case, requiring an understanding of its own particular logic, its own unique character."[8] War is the ultimate act of competition brought to its most violent finale. But competition does not have to have such an end in the modern world, when there is a very definite danger of all competitors becoming losers with catastrophic consequences for everyone involved. In general, Gerasimov's idea can also be expanded by assuming that each competition between civilizations or nation-states does in fact represent an isolated case. For each such isolated case of competition there are several ways of avoiding an ultimate, and terrifying outcome, that is to say—avoiding what Allison describes as the Thucydides Trap.

Such avoidance starts with understanding the nature of military power and of its application. This becomes absolutely crucial in such cases as the demolition of Saddam Hussein's Army by a coalition led by the U.S. Armed Forces in 1991. If whatever lessons of the Battle of Lepanto in the tactical and operational senses are inapplicable for the Battle of Midway or the Falklands War due to a massive technological gap, the same could be stated about the "lessons" of the First Gulf War which, generally, devolved into a turkey shoot of the vast undertrained Iraqi Army, which enjoyed no operational Air Force nor even a remotely capable Air Defense to speak of. In fact, any lessons from that war could and, in fact, did provide a baneful influence on the state of mind of many Western civilian and military leaders. Hubris and gross misinterpretation of the results occurred despite many professionals describing in depth the Iraqi Army's dramatic lack of capability, ranging from low quality of leaders and personnel, over-centralization of command, lack of ability for strategic assessment, lack of modern battle management means, not to mention gross technological inferiority.[9] As one observer pointed out:

> The Coalition exploited a superiority in every aspect of targeting, intelligence gathering and dissemination, integration of combined arms and multi-service forces, and night and all-weather warfare to achieve both a new tempo of operations and one far superior to that of Iraq.[10]

If any true strategic lessons should have been learned from that war, those must have been in exercising an extreme caution when projecting experiences fighting the enemy which should be used as an exhibit A of how not to fight the war in any military academy. As Anthony Cordesman pointed out:

> Future enemies are not likely to wait for the U.S. and other states to deploy their power projection forces, and there is a clear need to develop better forms of strategic mobility, prepositioning, and interoperability. Iraq did not exploit the limits in Western capability to rapidly deploy power projection forces, but there is no question that several months elapsed before the U.S. could deploy sufficient heavy land forces to ensure the forward defense of Saudi Arabia, and several more months elapsed before the U.S. could deploy large enough land forces to liberate Kuwait.[11]

In that statement Cordesman implicitly reveals the main reasons for the recent emergence of many pseudo-military and pseudo-historic intellectual constructs which range from that already being discussed here, the Thucydides Trap. to downright bizarre concepts such as *Tolerance Warfare,* which was described by its inventor, London International Institute for Strategic Studies (IISS) Director General John Chipman (holder of an MA from the London School of Economics and an Ph.D. from Balliol College Oxford), as follows:

> Tolerance warfare is the effort to push back lines of resistance, probe weaknesses, assert rights unilaterally, break rules, establish new facts on the ground, strip others of initiative and gain systematic advantage over hesitant opponents. It particularly exploits weaknesses in Western democracies whose instincts for statecraft have been tempered by geopolitical failure abroad and constraints imposed by domestic opinion

on hard-power international deployment. It is becoming a favored strategy for those countries that cannot easily challenge their biggest rivals symmetrically.[12]

Why Dr. Chipman decided that this description of classic conflict and warfare which has existed since the dawn of humanity and is always based on either exploitation of the enemy's weaknesses, or creating conditions for such exploitation, merits a new moniker remains a process primarily among Western political "scientists" who fail to recognize how military power shapes geopolitical reality. These are the same "scientists," such as Mark Galeotti, who came up with yet another simulacra of *Hybrid Warfare* while failing to recognize that any warfare is hybrid by definition since it involves employment of a vast variety of means ranging from kinetic to ideological psyops, intelligence, fiscal and economic warfare. History is filled with examples of such "hybrid warfare" from ancient times and it was and remains known as a war.

Yet, it seems, in the West, people who have degrees in anything but serious military and technological fields, and who, for the most part never served a day in uniform, let alone having any tactical or operational command experience have decided that they have enough intellectual wherewithal to pass judgements on the subject of war. The results today are what one might expect from such a mismatch between available and required skills for the scale of such a task as the study of warfare—the lack of any coherent answers or reliable forecasts and multiplication of essences, which, far from helping to understand warfare and military balance, aggravate confusion and serve no other purpose than the self-promotion of the people who invented them.

In general, modern warfare and global military balance are defined by a combination of complex economic, scientific, social, personal and myriad other factors among which technology and what it entails remains one of the most decisive ones. This is precisely the field which requires serious military and scientific-engineering backgrounds for people willing to speak on the subject to be able to have even a basic, not to mention a full understanding of the modern world and the way military power in general, and the military-industrial complex in particular, shape it. Studies of this are extremely important, in fact vital, for humanity's survival. Addressing this subject based on a constant regurgitation of old truths under new labels serves no practical purpose and, in fact, begins to exert unnecessary and pseudo-scholastic confusion in the already badly confused and, in many senses, incompetent Western field of political science which thinks that it knows what it preaches. It doesn't, and naming great power competition by bestowing on it the anti-scientific title of the Thucydides Trap does not change the nature of this competition and the urgent need for modern Western political "science" to get its own house in order for the single purpose of providing reliable and realistic forecasting instead of non-stop doctrine and terms mongering and working hard to make a fictional Thucydides Trap a geostrategic reality and worse, a self-fulfilling prophesy. This task, it seems, today is beyond the capability of contemporary Western think-tank-dom which is utterly unprepared for the realities of a new world which has a dramatic increase in military capabilities. Given this inadequacy, along with the emergence of a new military balance, American technological superiority is not only not guaranteed, but put into serious doubt.

This problem of technological incompetence is nothing new for Western political and intellectual classes. As General Latiff noted:

Make no mistake: the willful ignorance of the American public and its leaders will have dangerous consequences. Most Americans, including many of our political leaders, pay scant attention to military issues until a situation arises concerning our armed forces. Then they act based on emotion and political expedience rather than on facts, and that rarely ends well.[13]

As I stressed strongly in my previous work, *Losing Military Supremacy: The Myopia of American Strategic Planning,* American lack of historical experience with continental warfare and all the horrors it brings planted the seeds of the ultimate destruction of the American military mythology of the 20th and 21st centuries which is foundational to the American decline, due to hubris and detachment from the reality.[14] Such a process is not surprising in a society where, as Latiff states, much of what the public knows or thinks about the military derives from entertainment.[15] American entertainment depicts American military technology as a pinnacle of modern warfare, often ignoring the fact that this is no longer the case and that competitors do not sit idly by, accepting American declarations of its military superiority. It simply doesn't work like this, it never did. Even the most advanced technology malfunctions under the most lax conditions. Under conditions of serious counter-measures and a serious return of fire the dynamics of a modern battle can easily spin out of control and will make the use of the most advanced military technology very difficult, if possible at all. It is sufficient to consider what should be the response(s) to such an event as, say, the degrading of the capability of GPS, the main guidance correction tool in American arsenal for its cruise missiles. Such a degradation will inevitably lead to a dramatic loss of accuracy and with it a reduction in the effectiveness of strikes on the enemy. Sadly, these seemingly simple understandings are often beyond the grasp of U.S. policy makers who even need special explanations on such matters as why satellites cannot be moved at will into the desired orbit.[16] Explaining basic laws of modern war may turn into exercise in futility altogether since for a person with no serious academic military background the concepts of attrition, salvo, search or any other models used for the assessment of one's own and the enemy's kinetic capabilities, even in their basic form, are difficult to understand. But these models are not Hollywood imagery; rather they describe increasingly complex modern warfare, which is foundational to a competition between great powers.

Any "strategic" concept advanced by the Western political class, unless it is supported by a serious assessment of military power and its application, merits nothing more than the title of an exercise in sophistry and, as the last two decades demonstrated so dramatically, shouldn't be taken seriously—be that Fukuyama's "End of History," neoconservative war-mongering, liberal interventionism, Thucydides Trap, or even Huntington's most impressive effort. There is nothing scientific about those concepts without a deep understanding of the nature of military power. This very real military science is ignored by the majority of the Western political class, most of which is a product of humanities and social studies programs which do not even remotely provide any insight into the nature of the military-technological competition, which shaped and continues to shape our world addicted to warfare.

How, then, is it possible to avoid a global war when the elites who increasingly drive the world towards it are ignorant of the very nature of this war? One may, of course, exercise the illusion that teaching the decision-makers the basics of modern warfare will address this problem. It is doubtful, however, that the Western political class in general, and the

American one in particular, busy with their own reelections and pushing agendas to the benefit of their campaign contributors, will find the necessary—fairly long—time and energy to learn the basics of military analysis: even basic differential equations with separable variables require some good grasp of basic calculus, while effectiveness assessments or calculations of the required forces call for a decent understanding of the theory of probability. This is just for starters. Much more still is required to obtain a basic grasp of military power and balance.

Yet, educating the general public in such matters can help address at least some perception issues which originated in turning modern warfare into entertainment and, as a consequence, creating a grossly distorted image of war as a video game by Hollywood and writers like the late Tom Clancy who wrote about how things should work, not how they worked in actuality.[17] Modern war is an extremely complex affair, as is global military balance: educating the general public on this complexity and on the inherent non-linearity of war and of military balance thus becomes an extremely important task which may, in the end, discard all contrived theories and show war for what it is—a bloody, gruesome affair which brings only death, suffering and destruction.

CHAPTER 2

Measuring Geopolitical Power in Numbers: Why Existing Mathematical Models Fail

Of all the Western geopolitical concepts of the past 30 years, only Samuel Huntington's seminal *The Clash of Civilizations and the Remaking of World Order* made some scientific geopolitical sense, albeit providing few other astute insights that held well against the reality of the early 21st century, when it addressed Jeffrey R. Barnett's 14 reasons for the West's domination.[1] Most of those factors, 11 out of 14, are of purely industrial-technological, scientific and by implication, military nature. The reasoning here is extremely simple: to have a modern weapon, such as an artillery system, for example, produced in a completely enclosed technological cycle, from mining minerals, to processing them, to conducting R&D, to manufacturing such a weapon, a nation needs a developed economy. When speaking about the whole spectrum of very advanced weapon systems, from nuclear weapons to advanced combat aircraft to sensors, among many other systems, an economy on the scale of a superpower is required. This seems to go without saying for anyone who deals with advanced manufacturing and military. As it turns out, this kind of intuitive understanding is not always enjoyed by many decision makers, not to mention lay people. And in turn it becomes an altogether insurmountable intellectual feat for those who operate within the framework of monetary values and equate, wrongly, the cost of a weapon, and/or how it looks, with its capability. Aircraft Carriers undeniably provide outstanding visuals but modern warfare leaves very little place for these ships. The problem becomes even more aggravated when one has to understand how complex weapons are designed and especially how they are used, i.e. deployed—things get further complicated once one has to consider an enemy who, in accordance with the famous definition of a war as a democratic affair, has their say, too.

But even before that, one has to understand how the weaponry, even before being used, influences geopolitical reality through assumptions related to military power. This requires at least some modeling and calculations. It is in human nature to quantify things—nothing is wrong with that. Quantification allows us to see some order in what are otherwise seemingly chaotic processes. It also allows us to predict outcomes based on those quantifications. Sometimes predictions pan out but often they do not. As the events of the last 20 or so years showed us, no mathematical model, no matter how sophisticated, can properly predict the global strategic balance, even despite the availability of what has become known as "Big Data." Two realities prevent our trusting such a modeling fully:

1. It matters *what* data and *who* counts it. The famous meme of GIGO—Garbage In, Garbage Out did not appear out of nowhere. It suffices to recall the complete misinformation most U.S. pollsters were providing prior to the 2016 U.S. presidential elections. It illustrates the dreadful extent to which biases influence perceptions even in something as significant as electing Donald Trump to the highest political office of the nation.[2] Another example is WW II and how it was "interpreted" by the West, which convinced itself that it was the power which crushed Nazism—despite overwhelming empirical evidence to the contrary.

2. Anything related to strategy and military is inherently human at its very foundation, and as such it is stochastic

in nature, that is, susceptible to the introduction of random variables and those variables sometimes become the proverbial monkey wrench which messes up all, even perfect, assessments and plans. In the end, the data itself *must* be full and reliable—otherwise one gets the equivalent of Wall Street reports on the state of economy, which are as reliable and as connected to its actual reality as a fantasy novel.

Or, in a more specific example, U.S. President Obama was led to embarrass himself by declaring in 2015 that sanctions were leaving the Russian economy "in tatters."[3] Those observing this very Russian economy, after allegedly being left in tatters, is not only doing just fine, but in fact growing steadily, have to ask: based on what data was such a conclusion made? Presumably somebody did calculate some numbers for Obama, using some criteria which, as it turned out, were so out of touch with Russia's economic reality, and accidently with American economic reality, too, that Obama's phrase became a meme both in Russia and abroad. The answer to this puzzle of why President Obama produced such a grossly erroneous statement is twofold.

1. The economic and national power assessment criteria which dominate the top political echelons in the U.S. in general are either partially or completely wrong;

2. The economic data on both Russia, and the U.S. was wrong, and because of these wrong criteria, accumulated even more errors while being processed.

In other words, the models which were used are unreliable at best. This reliance on distorted modeling, as I stated in my previous work, *Losing Military Supremacy: The Myopia of American Strategic Planning,* is unique to the American political class since this class completely buys its own false narrative of American economic and military power exceptionalism and is not dealing well with the cognitive dissonances which manifest themselves with increasing frequency, proving its exceptionalism narrative wrong in a most dramatic, i.e. empirical, way. In the end, it is "facts on the ground," not abstract theories, which matter. Yet, when one is being critical of most theories on geopolitical balance, which by implication entails both economic and military considerations, one still has to have some tools which allow one to at least order and organize the immense stream of information available today in regard to economic, military, technological and other factors as described in Barnett's 14 points. There are, surely, some models which claim to provide such tools. While examining the specific instances of this modelling is beyond the scope of this book, a brief examination of the nature of such modeling is highly warranted.

Many people who are immersed in the 24-hour news cycle and try to follow the massive geopolitical changes unfolding in front of our very eyes on an hourly basis are bombarded by a barrage of allegedly scientific terms which are supposed to describe the current state of the world. The barrage ranges from terms such as *soft power, robust military response or operational tempo to soft demand, quantitative easing,* or other, often confusing, terms, many of which are just fancy names for understandable and even mundane processes and tasks. Yet, increasingly with the passage of time, no matter how one uses an increasing number of terms in trying to describe the modern world, it is becoming impossible to describe it without using numbers and beyond that, mathematical laws. What does powerful mean, how can one measure might, both economic and military, what is a capability— one must have basic mathematical apparatus to express at least some properties of the phenomena described by these terms. Nowhere does this necessity arise more dramatically than when dealing with what is military on any level, be it technological, tactical or doctrinal.

While President Trump may tout his "nice, new and smart" missiles such as the BGM-109 TLAM (Tomahawk Land Attack Missile) while ordering illegal strikes on Syria as he did in April of 2018, this was a grossly inaccurate description of what amounted to a venerable and yet ineffective weapon against even the moderately competent Syrian air-defense. As events demonstrated, these missiles could hardly be called new or smart by the standards of modern times. Even the *Washington Post* was forced to publish an explanation of what "smart" means in Donald Trump's description.[4] Yet, even the *Post's* very basic and inaccurate description, from the technological point of view—"missiles that use precision guidance systems based on lasers or satellite-powered GPS to pinpoint and strike targets with exactitude"—provides virtually zero useful information.[5] Nor would adding adjectives such as *very accurate or precise* contribute anything of descriptive value to this or any other weapon systems. It would be akin to describing the U.S. economy as the largest in the world, which in reality it is not, once actual verified and contextualized numbers are compared between the American and Chinese economies.[6] Mathematics projected on empirical data becomes very important and anyone wishing to have a more accurate picture of geopolitical reality has to face at least some basic math, because it is impossible to describe the world without it.

Lewis Fry Richardson (1881-1953), the British physicist, psychologist and pacifist, who applied mathematics in order to describe an arms race and produce models of conflicts, stated once:

> To have to translate one's own verbal statements into mathematical formulae compels one carefully to scrutinize the ideas therein expressed. Next, the possession of formulae makes it much easier to deduce the

consequences. In this way absurd implications, which might have passed unnoticed in a verbal statement, are brought clearly into view and stimulate one to amend the formula. An additional advantage of a mathematical model is its brevity, which greatly diminishes the labor of memorizing the idea expressed.[7]

We are not going to review Richardson's arms race model here—it is outdated and requires very serious quality adjusters to an otherwise purely quantity-driven model.[8] But one of the models which does reflect a degree of competition and is helpful in gaining an understanding of equilibrium between major powers that Richardson was trying to describe is the model, *Status of the Nation*. This model is claimed to be quantitative and is new despite absorbing many principles of geopolitics and military balance from as far back in time as the work of Alfred Thayer Mahan up to the 2005 RAND publication, *Measuring National Power*. This model, developed within the framework of the project *Complex System Analysis and Modelling of Global Dynamics,* which was done in the world-renowned Keldysh Institute of Applied Mathematics of Russian Academy of Sciences was developed by a group of researchers who titled their paper "Russia in the Context of World's Geopolitical Dynamics: Quantitative Assessment of Historic Retrospective, Current State and Perspectives for Development."[9]

This model is very instructive for a number of reasons, the main one being a manifest failure in accounting for qualitative, such as operational and technological, military factors as the main drivers of the geopolitical balance and status of nations. Yet, it is a useful model having given some framework for geopolitical analysis. Don't be afraid of the mathematics which follows, it is deliberately reduced in complexity to a level of very basic middle-school math and is not going to introduce any calculus, however basic. We also use here rather approximate values from different sources and the calculations are deliberately given in a detailed step-by-step manner in order to allow the reader to use his or her numbers instead, taken from open sources. It has to be stated, however, that a variation of those values will not alter the general impression of final values and ratios by much. In other words, feel free to play with the numbers; in fact—it is highly recommended that you do so in order to get a feel for how the different ratios change. In the end, introduce your own imaginary absurd numbers, those will allow you to push the envelope of the model and see pattern.

The model states that the status of any nation can be calculated by a very simple formula:

$$S(t) = F_A(t)G(t)$$

where $S(t)$ is the status at a given point of time, $F_A(t)$ is the "function of influence" which accounts for combined influence of factors not connected to geopolitical potential and $G(t)$ is a geopolitical potential which has its own formula.[10] As you can see, the model is extremely simple—it is a product between numerical value, at given time of function of influence and of geopolitical potential. In other words, if one has function of influence $F_A(t)$ equaling 5 and geopolitical potential $G(t)$ equaling 3 for some nation, then the status of this nation $S(t)$ will equal 5 x 3 = 15. Obviously, in and of itself this number is absolutely meaningless unless it is compared to other numbers for other nations' $S(t)$. The question now is—how to calculate those. We may start with $F_A(t)$ and immediately point out its reasonable methodology but also its dramatic vulnerability to misinterpretations.

As was stated before, $F_A(t)$ which is the "function of influence," is not exactly related to geopolitical potential. It accounts for such factors as the quality of the state's management, its economic and military independence, plus the power-up the nation gets for entering a military-political coalition.[11] All those factors then are multiplied to get a numeric value of $F_A(t)$. It is worth venturing into this formula:

$$F_A(t) = (1-k_u)^{0.11} \cdot (1-\tfrac{J}{Y})^{0.27} \cdot (1-\tfrac{W_a}{W_g+W_a})^{0.43} \cdot (1+\tfrac{n_b}{N_B} \sum_{i=1}^{n_b} G_i)$$

Don't be intimidated by this seemingly large formula— you know all values in it and, in fact, if you are reading this book, you deal with those numbers very often one way or another, because even rudimentary interest in the military balance requires operating with these numbers, which are widely available in public domain, be that media or numerous special reports on economy and military balance. So, in this equation:

k_u—is a parameter of state's management which is defined by experts and we are experts here and we can define this factor later;

J—is the volume of import;

Y—is the nation's GDP;

W_g—is the number of foreign troops on the state's territory;

W_a—is the number of its own troops (size of the army) on the state's territory;

n_b—is the number of member-nations of the particular military-political bloc;

N_B—is the overall number of member-nations of different military-political blocs or coalitions;

G_i—is the geopolitical potential of any given member-nation in a particular coalition with sigma notation $\sum$ signifying the sum of potentials of all members of the coalition.

Let's consider a rough calculation of the function of influence for a couple of nations. The People's Republic of China and the United States will do with the relevant numbers extracted from the public domain. You will need a scientific calculator with the button y^x for easy handling of the decimal exponents. It is important to note, however, that we have dramatically simplified this model in order to obtain very rough estimates for educational purpose and to avoid getting into a more complex mathematical framework. We may start with China:

China's Function of Influence:[12]

k_u—is a parameter of state's management. Here, for the sake of simplification, we simply introduce for both the U.S. and China the same number, which is 0.5, even though there is a case to be made for China having a better, i.e. smaller, state management parameter, than that of the United States for a number of political and economic reasons, especially when one observes a complete gridlock of the U.S. political system.

J—is the volume of import. For China this number, in grossly inaccurate U.S. Dollar representation, for the year 2018 is $1.784 trillion.

Y—is the nation's GDP. Here we completely discard any nominal, grossly inaccurate, GDP and use China's PPP (Purchase Power Parity) GDP which is $15.309 trillion.

W_a—is the number of foreign troops on the state's territory. For China this number equals 0 since there are no foreign troops on China's territory. However, because the equation must account for a coalition deployment of troops, otherwise the Influence Function will equal zero and becomes meaningless, we introduce for both China and the U.S., which also has no foreign troops on its territory, an equal number of virtual foreign troops on their territory—25,000 each.

W_a—is the number of its own troops (size of the army) on the state's territory. We use here simply the size of the

Chinese PLA (People Liberation Army), that is, the number of active personnel, which is roughly 2,000, 000.[13]

The last two parameters could be reduced to:

n_b—is the number of member-nations of the particular military-political bloc. For China this number will be 1 since China is not a member of any particular bloc.

N_B—is the overall number of member-nations of different military-political blocks or coalitions. In our case China will have to contend with the fact that in the U.S., Japan, Australia and New Zealand, she faces four nations which do represent a coalition, so here the number is going to be 4.

We immediately run here into the problem of having to have a value for China's G_i, or for that matter, for all other members of the opposing coalition, such as the United States, Japan, Australia etc. This number is yet to be found, but even without such a number we can already calculate most of the equation. We simply plug in our numbers:

$$F_A(t) = (1-0.5)^{0.11} \cdot (1 - \tfrac{1.784}{15.309})^{0.27} \cdot (1 - \tfrac{2,000,000}{2,025,000})^{0.43} \cdot (1 + \tfrac{1}{4} G_{china})$$

Or to simplify:

$$F_A(t) = 0.5^{0.11} \cdot 0.8835^{0.27} \cdot 0.01235^{0.43} \cdot (1 + 0.25 G_{china})$$

$$= 0.1355 + 0.033875 G_{china}$$

Now we can calculate the same for the United States, only here we are going to accept the economic numbers as true.

United States' Function of Influence:

$k_u = 0.5$

J—is the volume of import, which is \$2.16 trillion, making the U.S. the largest importer in the world.[14]

Y—is the nation's GDP. It is claimed that it is \$19.391 trillion.

W_g—25,000.

W_a—is the number of its own troops (size of the army) on the state's territory. We use here simply the size of the U.S. Armed Forces, that is, the number of active personnel, which is roughly 1,360, 000 per Wikipedia.

The last two parameters could be reduced to:

n_b—is the number of —member-nations of the particular military-political bloc; for the U.S. we assume this number to be 4.

N_B—is the overall number of member-nations of different military-political blocks or coalitions, in our case it is going to be 1, meaning China.

Here is how the United States will look like in its Function of Influence when compared to China:

$$F_A(t) = (1-0.5)^{0.11} \cdot (1 - \tfrac{2.16}{19.391})^{0.27} \cdot (1 - \tfrac{2,000,000}{2,025,000})^{0.43} \cdot (1 + \tfrac{4}{1}\sum G_i)$$

We simplify:

$$F_A(t) = 0.5^{0.11} \cdot 0.8886^{0.27} \cdot 0.01235^{0.43} \cdot (1 + 4(G_{us} + G_{jpn} + G_{aus} + G_{nz})) =$$

$$= 0.1357 + 0.5428(G_{us} + G_{jpn} + G_{aus} + G_{nz})$$

Even a brief review of numbers seems to indicate that the United States, adjusted for the coalition factor, is much more powerful than China. But here is where the model actually begins to fail. Even before we calculate the crucial multiple in the Status Model of the geopolitical potential of the nation $G(t)$, we can make a few legitimate assumptions in case of a serious conflict between the United States and China which will change the function of influence $F_A(t)$ for both nations rather dramatically.

1. In the case of serious and escalating conflict between two nuclear superpowers it is not out of the realm of the possible—in fact, it is highly probable—that the American "coalition" nations, be they Japan or Australia, will have huge reservations about direct participation in such a conflict, thus reducing the factor of $(1+\frac{4}{1}\sum G_i)$ in American case to roughly $(1+G_{us})$ and the same for China $(1+G_{china})$. In other words it is going to be primarily a dyadic U.S.-China conflict with most potential allies trying to stay away and observe from afar.

2. Data about the U.S. economy is notoriously unreliable and does not reflect the actual state which matters most of all for a conflict—its manufacturing, all kinds of it. If the colossal number of the American imports, $2.16 trillion, is any indication, as well as the precipitous decline of American machine building, one is forced to seriously adjust one's views of the American economy.

As the September 2018 Interagency Report on American Manufacturing to President Trump underscores:

> The U.S. machine tools sector lacks assured access to a sufficiently large pool of skilled labor. Many skilled workers are exiting the workforce due to age, and there are too few technical educational programs to train those who could take their place. Without concerted action that provides both a ready workforce and a continuously-charged pipeline of new employees, the U.S. will not be able to maintain the large, vibrant, and diverse machine tools sector needed to produce the required number and types of products when needed. The U.S. machine tools sector has been shrinking since

at least the 1980s due to a number of primary and contributing factors with the U.S. standing dropping significantly since 2000. In 2015, China's global machine tool production skyrocketed to $24.7B accounting for 28% of global production, while the U.S. accounted for only $4.6B, after China, Japan, Germany, Italy, and South Korea. According to the U.S. Census Bureau data, in 2015 there were 1,028 machine tool firms employing 27,919 people.[15]

Expressed in U.S. Dollars, the American share of manufacturing in her GDP is around $2.125 trillion.[16] China's manufacturing numbers are not consistent, yet as the CIA reports, China is a "world leader in gross value of industrial output."[17] It is precisely this output which matters most and which defines a nation's economy. In this respect the United States fell behind China—this changes the power balance calculus dramatically and not in the U.S. favor. And even when using grossly unreliable numbers for the American economy, our calculations for the function of influence still becomes:

For China:

$$F_A(t) = 0.5^{0.11} \cdot 0.8835^{0.27} \cdot 0.01235^{0.43} \cdot (1 + G_{china}) =$$
$$= 0.1355 + 0.1355 G_{china}$$

For the United States:

$$F_A(t) = 0.5^{0.11} \cdot 0.8835^{0.27} \cdot 0.01235^{0.43} \cdot (1 + G_{us}) =$$
$$= 0.1357 + 0.1357 G_{us}$$

And even this virtual parity between the two does not reflect the real relation between their respective influence functions. Considering China's monstrous $382 billion positive trade balance with the U.S., and China's being the de facto global manufacturing powerhouse, it is entirely legitimate to

judge the value of China's influence function as much greater than that of the U.S.[18] This conclusion also follows from
the fact that the actual American GDP is formed primarily by
non-productive sectors such as finance and services known
as the FIRE economy. That explains the consistent pattern of
the ever increasing overall trade deficit for the United States
in the last few years.[19] This means, in other words, that the
actual size of the American economy is grossly inflated,
which is done for a number of reasons primarily related to
the status of the U.S. Dollar as reserve currency and the main
engine for its proliferation the Federal Reserve printing press
in the U.S. which has long lived beyond its means and is facing a dramatic devaluation of its status, as dedollarization of
world economy becomes a mainstream endeavor, in which
Russia leads the way.[20] In the end, China's real GDP, when
adjusted for still inaccurate, but much more reliable than
nominal, PPP (Purchase Power Parity) is dramatically larger
than the United States' GDP. China's GDP is projected by
some sources to be almost $27.5 trillion in 2019.[21] It is by a
full third greater than the claimed U.S. GDP; in reality, most
likely China's GDP is even greater when GDP is viewed
primarily as a productive, that is, real economy, index.

That brings us to this ever important issue of Russia and
her function of influence. It is undeniable that Russia's GDP
is much smaller than that of the United States and China.
It is also clear that it is much larger than as viewed by traditional Western financial assessments. In the end even the
International Monetary Fund projects Russia's GDP to reach
roughly $4.2 trillion in 2019.[22] In this case Russia's function
of influence is relatively easy to calculate, once one considers
the same assumptions on coalitions as was done when comparing China and America's functions. Management factor
k_u for Russia is reduced somewhat, thus giving Russia an
advantage in this category, once one considers conditions

under which Russia exists and develops—a testimony to a very high level of state management:

$$F_A(t) = (1-0.3)^{0.11} \cdot (1 - \tfrac{0.182}{4.2})^{0.27} \cdot (1 - \tfrac{1,013,000}{1,038,000})^{0.43} \cdot (1 + G_{Russia})$$

$$F_A(t) = 0.7^{0.11} \cdot 0.95666^{0.27} \cdot 0.02408^{0.43} \cdot (1 + G_{Russia}) =$$

$$= 0.19138 + 0.19138 G_{Russia}$$

This number seems intuitively wrong, because Russia's function of influence cannot be larger than that of China and the U.S., which are much larger economically than Russia. The multiplier $0.19138 G_{Russia}$ completely ignores the fact of Russia facing virtually alone—if one discounts the important but not completely reliable addition of the Republic of Belarus—the entire military and economies of the largest coalition in history; NATO. Once this is factored in, the value of Russia's function of influence will be diminished greatly and it will fall below that of China and, especially, that of the United States which, for all intents and purposes, is NATO, with the rest of this military-political block being merely subordinate appendices.

We should, however, keep in mind that this function of influence is just one out of two multipliers which constitute geopolitical status. The second multiplier is $G(t)$ which stands for geopolitical potential of the nation. This is precisely where the real dramatic breakdown of the model happens, thus throwing the entire model in disarray. The reason for that is a straightforward one—military potential cannot be measured purely quantitatively; it requires serious qualitative adjustments. This is where it makes total sense to demonstrate the breakdown of the model. In the end, influences, same as reputations, are difficult to build and are very easy to lose. Potentials, however, are more durable and an easier to comprehend commodity.

The formula for the geopolitical potential of the nation looks like this:

$$G(t) = 0.5(1 + X_M^{0.43})X_T^{0.11}X_D^{0.19}X_E^{0.27}$$

In this formula Xs with subscripts stand for shares of the nation in global indices of: M-military, T-territory, D-demography, E-economies. The numbers above are exponents or the power to which those indices must be raised. Here, the calculations are pretty straightforward when dealing with territory, demography, and if properly adjusted, economy. The military index, however, is the most difficult of all in this Status Model since military power is an elusive concept which cannot be directly quantified without a danger of losing the recognition of the most important transition of quantity into quality and vice versa. And as in the previous example with function of influence, where we left G_{China}, G_{US} and G_{Russia} as unknowns, we will have to do the same to X_M which is supposed to be the share of the global military power. But expressed in what metric?

It is very easy to calculate, approximately as it is, all others but the military shares. Indeed, the United States' population is 322 million, China's—1,404 million. Consequently the shares in the global population are as follows: U.S.—4.31% of total population (we use the round number of 7,467 million for the World's total population) and China's—18.8%. The same goes for economies in monetary expression: GDP is taken per the CIA World Fact book, U.S.—$19.36 trillion, China—$23.12. Consequently the shares in the global GDP are as follows: U.S.—15.24% of total GDP and China—18.2%. Again, we use CIA's round number of $127 trillion for the World's total GDP. Territory wise: the territory for the U.S. is almost the same as China's, 9.147 million square kilometers for the U.S. and 9.326 million square kilometers for China. Consequently the shares in the global territory are as follows: U.S.—6.13% of global land mass and China—6.26%. We use the round number of 149 million square kilometers for the World's total land mass.

For Russia, the numbers, as shares, will be:

$$X_T = \frac{17.125}{149} = 11.5\%$$

$$X_D = \frac{147}{7,467} = 1.96\%$$

$$X_E = \frac{4.2}{127} = 3.3\%$$

So, we can now calculate the Geopolitical Potentials:
For the United States for 2019 Geopolitical Potential will look like this:

$$G(2019)_{US} = 0.5(1 + X_M^{0.43})6.13^{0.11}4.31^{0.19}15.24^{0.27} =$$
$$= 0.5(1 + X_M^{0.43})1.22 \cdot 1.32 \cdot 2.086 = 1.6796(1 + X_M^{0.43})$$

For China:

$$G(2019)_{China} = 0.5(1 + X_M^{0.43})6.26^{0.11}18.8^{0.19}18.2^{0.27} =$$
$$= 0.5(1 + X_M^{0.43})1.22 \cdot 1.75 \cdot 2.19 = 2.3378(1 + X_M^{0.43})$$

For Russia:

$$G(2019)_{Russia} = 0.5(1 + X_M^{0.43})11.5^{0.11}1.96^{0.19}3.3^{0.27} =$$
$$= 0.5(1 + X_M^{0.43})1.31 \cdot 1.14 \cdot 1.38 = 1.03(1 + X_M^{0.43})$$

It cannot fail to attract one's attention that the still unknown value of the share of the military $X_M^{0.43}$ has the largest exponent (power) of all the other shares constituting geopolitical potential—even larger than the economy, let alone territory or demographic values. This is correct in general sense, but what is the metric, the unit, of this share? It absolutely cannot be financial as expressed in military budgets.

In fact, using the financial metric is what has created the grossly distorted and "exceptionalist"—thus very dangerous—delusion on the part of many American thinkers and policy-makers who have equated the size of the mammoth American military budget with its military capability.

Many military analysts have started to depart from the false financial criteria when assessing military power and to gravitate towards actual military capability. As U.S. Marine Corps captain, a veteran of American wars, Joshua Waddell noted:

> Judging military capability by the metric of defense expenditures is a false equivalency. All that matters are raw, quantifiable capabilities and measures of effectiveness. For example: a multi-billion dollar aircraft carrier that can be bested by a few million dollars in the form of a swarming missile barrage or a small unmanned aircraft system (UAS) capable of rendering its flight deck unusable does not retain its dollar value in real terms. Neither does the M1A1 tank, which is defeated by $20 worth of household items and scrap metal rendered into an explosively-formed projectile. The Joint Improvised Threat Defeat Organization has a library full of examples like these, and that is without touching the weaponized return on investment in terms of industrial output and capability development currently being employed by our conventional adversaries.[23]

So what, then, is this military capability X_M which plays such a preeminent role in the model of geopolitical capability? The formula for it is, yet again, rather simple. It is:

$$X_M = 0.5 X_{M1}[0.5(X_{M2} + X_{M3}) + X_{M4}]$$

where M1 is the share of the nation in global military ex-penditures, M2 is the military potential of the nation's Army, M3 is the military potential of the nation's Navy and, finally, M4 is the potential of its strategic nuclear forces. As you can see, the authors of this model still persevere in using military expenditures as one of the main indices, and this is precisely where this model begins to fail dramatically. The United States spends more on national defense than China, Russia, Saudi Arabia, India, France, the United Kingdom, and Japan combined.[24] Yet, despite this astonishing number it is absolutely clear for any sober-headed observer that the United States is on a continuous downward spiral of dimin-ishing military capabilities against the nation she thought she defeated in the Cold War. Quantitative models, of course, are necessary as one of the tools which allows to get a different perspective in the issues related to any capability, but what may work in economics or other fields does not describe a complex reality of warfare and military balance. We will review why in the next chapters.

CHAPTER 3

How to (Really) View Warfare in Numbers

The purely quantitative, in effect linear, approach to measuring a nation's military potential[1] has a major drawback—it doesn't work. But that is precisely what makes the use of such a restrictive model highly instructive in pointing out how *not* to assess either geopolitical status or military potential. Why failure, then? I, and many other military professionals, have raised this issue many times, pointing out that pure dollar-for-dollar comparison of military expenditures (M1) is a false equivalency. The problem here is not just with proverbial bang for a buck, in which the greatest military spender, the United States, does not get as much as any other of its nearest competitors for its buck. After all, for the price of a single, and still on the drawing boards, U.S. strategic missile submarine (SSBN) of the future *Columbia-class,* the Russian Navy paid for eight state of the art and very real strategic missile submarines of the project 955(A), known as *Borei-class.*[2] Three out of those eight submarines are already operational.

The costs of the SSBNs, of course, cannot serve even remotely as a famous Big Mac index to be used to give an impression of the purchasing power of different currencies but it is still quite a remarkable ratio once one gets to comprehend this simple fact: Russia builds a close equivalent of the U.S. prospective *Columbia-class* SSBN for roughly one eighth of the *Columbia's* cost. So it seems reasonable to assume that a serious "shrinking" factor must be introduced when considering the astronomical U.S. military budget of roughly $700 billion as a measure of its military power.[3] To what extent could this shrinking be? Certainly not by one eighth, which would adjust $700 billion to roughly $87.5 billion. But furthermore, account must be taken of the fact that the United States buys very expensive military technology which clearly does not necessarily deliver superior military capability. In other words, the issue is not just quantitative, it is qualitative and doctrinal.

In 1976, while speaking to Joseph C. Harsch of the *Christian Science Monitor,* Admiral Stansfield Turner, then NATO Commander for Southern Europe, delivered with the clarity of a top level professional one of the most important doctrinal truisms. Responding to the question on whose navy, Soviet or American, was better, Turner replied: "It isn't the number of keels, or size of ships that count. It is the capacity to do what might be decisive in some particular situation." Turner elaborated: "The big carrier is vulnerable to a long-range missile blow. So, the great American superiority in a 'projection of power ashore' counts heavily in situations short of Soviet-American war, but counts for almost nothing in such a war."[4]

The United States spends astronomical sums, numbering in tens of billions of dollars, for building its power projection forces, at the heart of which are prohibitively expensive nuclear aircraft carriers (CVNs) and amphibious ships. While Russia doesn't do anything like this, she does build weapons which can guarantee the defeat of such forces in case of a Russian-American war. Russia does it for a fraction of the cost and by so doing, changed warfare forever. The model derived in the previous chapter[5] cannot account for it, even when the status of Russia with or without nuclear weapons' limitations imposed by existing and possibly future treaties is taken into account, greatly diminishing the status of Russia, in the case of Strategic Weapons

Limitations negotiations succeeding. But even with Russia retaining her present status, not constrained or reduced by limitation treaties, authors measuring nuclear arsenal capability still predicted Russia's status as steadily declining over the years.[6] Not only were the authors and their model wrong, but after President Vladimir Putin's March 1, 2018 Address to Russia's Federal Assembly, it became irrelevant. To understand why this and many other similar models fail, one has to take a brief review of the mathematics of real warfare—without it, no military or geopolitical power model will ever succeed in predicting both geopolitical status of a nation and global military balance. Effectiveness of killing the enemy is what must be viewed as the most important criterion in geopolitical balance.

The Theory of Operations, Measuring Attrition:
A Brief Review

In 1915 Russian mathematician Mikhail Osipov wrote a series of articles generally known as *Estimation of the Numbers of Victims of War* where he offered an attrition model which was based on two differential equations, which measured the proportionality of combat losses to the size of the opposite force. Year later, in 1916, English engineer Frederik Lanchester came up with the same model as Osipov, though eventually the laws described by both became known as the Lanchester Laws.[7] This attrition model in its simplest form looks like this:

$$\begin{cases} \frac{dA}{dt} = -B \\ \frac{dB}{dt} = -A \end{cases}$$

where A and B are the numbers of respective opposing forces, while d is change in numbers and t is time. So, let us conduct a mental experiment: let us model the simple battle, or shoot-out. Imagine we have two opposing forces, A and

B. Both forces are an exact match in terms of their weapons and skills, except for their numbers. Let's assume that force A has 1000 riflemen while force B has 750. These forces begin to shoot at each other and the intuitive and uninformed conclusion would be that, by the time A and B stop shooting at each other, force A will have 1000-750=250 riflemen left after completely annihilating force B. After all, force A is simply more numerous than force B by 250 riflemen. But: this is the wrong conclusion and not how it will most likely play out under the simplest conditions. Here is where the Lanchester-Osipov Laws come into play.

While arithmetic intuition may tell us that force A has to have 250 riflemen left after the shoot-out with force B, it doesn't take a mathematical mind to recognize that this crucial 250 riflemen difference in favor of force A will enable it to concentrate its fire on force B fully engaged in the shoot-out with 750 riflemen of 1000-strong force A, thus increasingly diminishing the *productivity* of force A, a factor which will increase non-linearly. To describe what really happens in the time period in which the respective forces will be shooting at each-other, we must transform our system of equations. But let us simplify these equations even more, by rewriting what dA and dB really are. They are nothing more than the difference, or change, between the numbers of respective forces before (start) and after (end) the battle, in our particular problem.

$$dA = A_{start} - A_{end}$$
$$dB = B_{start} - B_{end}$$

In other words $\frac{dA}{dt}$ and $\frac{dB}{dt}$ are also rates of losses, or attrition, of respective forces. Thus, combining our equations, we can rewrite our system as:

$$\begin{cases} A_{start} - A_{end} = -Bdt \\ B_{start} - B_{end} = -Adt \end{cases}$$

We want to know when both forces will reach zero in their strength, which can be expressed as: $-Bdt = 0$ and $-Adt = 0$, thus:

$$-Bdt = -Adt$$

This is the equation we want, because it allows us to integrate it for time of the battle, the time of the start and the time of the end. Those more familiar with simple calculus can remember now that taking a simplest integral is finding the antiderivative and then calculating the difference of its values on upper and lower limits of integration. In our cases these are times of start and finish. After integration of both sides of the equation 4 we arrive to equation which looks like this:

$$(B_{start}^2 - B_{end}^2) = (A_{start}^2 - A_{end}^2)$$

Consider this simple problem: we know that combat efficiency of the machine gunner equals combat efficiency of 36 riflemen. How many machine gunners will we need to completely substitute 1000 riflemen? No, it is not 1000 divided by 36 or nearly 28, it is 1000 divided by the square root of 36 which is 6. 1000/6 gives us about 167 machine gunners. That means that combat strength of a fighting force is calculated by multiplication of combat efficiency of a single unit (rifleman, squad, platoon, etc.) by the square of numerical strength. In layman's lingo it means one very important thing: the more numbers you have (let alone when you have numbers more effective than that of your enemy), the more disproportionate will be the distribution of losses in your favor. Indeed, recalculate this same problem but now 2,000 against 750. You will lose roughly 146 of your riflemen, that is 1854 of your troops will survive the battle. Some additional elaborations on a quadratic nature of Lanchester Model you can find in the endnotes for this chapter.[8]

Apart from sophisticated tactics, these days one can always consider the addition of airpower and stand-off weaponry to increase combat effectiveness. It is at this juncture that the Lanchester equations become increasingly complex and begin to account for a number of tactical and operational factors which cover such things as territory, the density of troops and the number of troops at the line of a direct combat engagement, among others. These forms of Lanchester Model are beyond the scope of this book and they deal with a dynamic of change of different variables involved with Lanchester equations. The Lanchester Model with its derivative Square Law found its empirical, albeit controversial, verification in such battles as the Battle of Iwo Jima and even the American Civil War attrition study by H.K. Weiss.[9] There were, however, other studies which concluded that the Lanchester Model is not a good tool for predicting losses, especially for a protracted battle and battles of different intensity. Yet, the Lanchester Model's significance is precisely in demonstrating mathematically the non-linear nature of warfare and the complex factors which shape it, including the qualitative parameters of opposing troops.

Even these simple calculations lead us to a very fundamental conclusion which is one of the main principles of war—the principle of the concentration of forces. While this principle is nothing new in warfare, the German Blitzkrieg and Soviet offensive operations of WW II presented a dramatic demonstration of its correctness when relatively narrow sectors of the front saw an immense concentration of troops and combat equipment in order to break through enemy defenses to strike to operational and strategic depths. In the Battle of Stalingrad, with the unfolding Soviet offensive (Operation *Uranus*) on November 19, 1942, Red Army forces concentrated three armies, one of them a tank army, against the single Romanian Third Army, thus achieving a numerical and qualitative advantage which resulted in a breakthrough and the eventual annihilation of the German, Italian, Hungarian and Romanian armies in the bloodiest battle of WWII.[10]

Of course, it seems simply intuitive that larger numbers should win or, using a maxim often misattributed to Stalin: quantity has a quality of its own. It is true, numbers do matter but qualitative factors, sometimes expressed as quantitative ones, grow in importance on an exponential scale whenever the modern combined arms warfare is invoked. In the end, the demolition of the Saddam's Army in 1991 was achieved primarily by the overwhelming advantage in quality of the U.S. Armed Forces, with the Coalition's substantial numerical advantage playing an important role but subordinate to quality, quality being the ability to kill many more times the enemy than vice-versa. As with the example given above of a special operations force fighting a numerically superior militia, one can address, even within a simple Quadratic Law attrition model, the issue of quality by attaching one or two attack helicopters to this special ops force that will shift the balance dramatically because of the helicopters' firepower, which would increase special ops' α drastically, thus ensuring that 40 special ops fighters can deal effectively with an 180-fighters strong, and even larger, militia force with little attrition for themselves.

As Russian operations against terrorists in Syria demonstrated, the use of precision guided stand-off weaponry such as cruise missiles of *X-101* or *3M14* (of *Kalibr* family) variety, makes the job of special forces much easier by striking the terrorists' positions, compounds and other places of their concentration, before special operations professionals mop up. One should not forget the contribution of a direct Close Air Support by attack planes and helicopters. That is added quality. In warfare, quality is the factor enabling the destruction of more enemy with the least attrition to oneself.

That brings us to the ever important issue of how to kill the enemy. The Lanchester Model is one of a few other models which are primarily used to describe ground warfare. And even here we are approaching a moment in history when the simple Lanchester Model breaks down for warfare conducted by advanced states with cutting-edge militaries. In such a conflict the meaning of attrition changes because modern warfare is primarily network-centered and a stand-off precision–guided-weapons driven affair. This absolutely doesn't mean, as many predicted, the end of traditional combined arms warfare—conventional, non-nuclear warfare by large formations is by no means dead or obsolete. Far from it, after the disastrous Russian Armed Forces reforms implemented by former Minister of Defense Anatoly Serdyukov, who was cheered on by a choir of largely incompetent military "experts" from Russia's so-called liberal camp, a dramatic return of Russian ground forces to a division structure and re-constituting of such formations as armies at Russia's Western borders testify to the vitality of a large-scale conventional option.[11]

This rethinking of combined arms warfare by Russia is not accidental. Not surprisingly, and prudently, Russia sees NATO—which is primarily a force controlled by and directed towards the promotion of United States interests with the rest of NATO members being merely subordinate appendages—as a viable threat at her borders and therefore of necessity chooses to also have a force which can fight and defeat any combination of threats emanating from the NATO Alliance in a conventional war. Unlike Iraq, however, Russia possesses conventional weapons which are designed to strike to operational and strategic depth not only in Europe but in North America, thus providing a serious conventional, not to speak of nuclear, deterrent against any attempts on Russia and her vicinity. The increasing nuclearization of American military doctrine, a dramatic departure from 1990s and 2000s when American conventional omnipotence was explicitly declared on many occasions, is a vivid illustration of the dawning realization of the tectonic shift in the nature of warfare.

Even brief comparisons of the stated objectives of the U.S. Nuclear Posture Reviews (NPRs) from 2010 and 2018 provide startling evidence of the American drift towards nuclear weapons, a position increasingly reminiscent of Russia's pattern of reliance on nuclear deterrence in the 1990s, when Russia's conventional forces had been all but demolished by the incompetent and criminal governance of the Yeltsin regime. The 2010 NPR had clearly laid out as one of its main objectives a reduction of the role of the nuclear weapons.[12] This proposed reduction was not due to then President Obama's general apprehension in regards to nuclear weapons, nor to any set of prudent attitudes by American policy-makers. Rather, it was primarily due to the confidence of the U.S. national security establishment in America's conventional prowess—the exact American posture predicted in 2008 by Russia's famed chief designer of nuclear missile technology Yuri Solomonov.[13] Yet, ten years later, in the 2018 NPR, nuclear weapons are still listed as a prime "hedge against an uncertain future."[14] The main reason for this shift is a recognition of the revolutionary change in warfare, which created circumstances in which the U.S. Armed Forces are not guaranteed to kill more efficiently and, in fact, would rather be the ones with greater rates of attrition than their enemy.

This state of the affairs was achieved by the Russian ability to attack key military infrastructure which for the last several decades had been considered by the United States both as crucial for the command and control of its forces and as untouchable, primarily due to the fact that the types of enemy the U.S. forces fought were entirely incapable of striking to its operational and strategic depths. This is no longer the case once Russia, in October 2015, launched both the 5,000+ kilometer range capable *X-101* and the 2,500-kilometer range capable *3M14* cruise missiles at terrorist targets in Syria from deep within in Russia's territory. This was the launch heard and viewed around the world.

The significance of this launch, beyond its pure propaganda value, however important, was due to the fact that every single NATO and U.S. installation in Europe, Middle East and parts of North America was now within the range of a salvo of Russian cruise missiles, in both the conventional and nuclear variants. For the first time in history NATO was under purely conventional, non-ballistic, threat, including a definite possibility of its troops' formations to be under sustained fire impact in their staging areas and on the march. This was not a paradigm shift many in NATO, blinded by their own propaganda and hubris, had expected.

If a case could have been made for the possibility, however improbable, of an intercept of salvos of low-flying, subsonic, stealthy cruise missiles by U.S. air-defense complexes, after Vladimir Putin's address to the Federal Assembly on March 1st, 2018 the whole warfare paradigm changed in a fully revolutionary manner. At that time, I described it as follows:

> Putin's message was clear: "You didn't listen to us then, you will listen to us now." After that he proceeded with what can only be described as a military-technological Pearl-Harbor meets Stalingrad. The strategic ramifications of the latest weapon systems Putin presented are immense. In fact, they are historic in nature.[15]

The introduction of the Lanchester Model above was important to give a sense of some of the basic numerical framework for ground warfare by providing a limited insight into the attrition of opposing forces. But while attrition rates are extremely important for analysis and assessment, they are not, by far, the only metric which is used to forecast the probabilities in warfare. Moreover, in a naval combat, insofar as it is fought by large, easily incrementable objects, attrition rates account for losses of ships and submarines. Naturally, the units of naval forces are far less numerous than even medium-size ground units. The Lanchester Model doesn't work in this particular case. Cases such as surface Fleet Against Fleet are calculated within the Salvo Combat Model which, due to the efforts of its brilliant inventor, Captain Wayne Hughes, emerged as a response to the increasing importance of anti-shipping cruise missiles pioneered by the Soviet Navy.

The Salvo Combat Model, like the Lanchester model, is based on attrition, this time of the number of ships put out of action by a salvo of cruise missiles by an opponent.[16] One may reasonably ask why this Model is specifically a missile model. The answer is easy enough—anti-shipping cruise missiles, unlike artillery shells of the battleship era, or for that matter bullets and shells of the field artillery in ground combat, can be actively countered by a defender. Missiles could be shot down, they could be deflected or completely disabled due to Electronic Counter Measures of a defender.

Of course, the non-augmented version of the Salvo Model presented here (see endnote 16) is rather simple, when compared to a much more comprehensive augmented version of it, which does account for a variety of tactical and operational factors such as readiness, training, effectiveness of countermeasures, and effectiveness of scouting, among a few others, which complicate matters significantly but give a much more realistic picture of the combat engagement. Yet, even in its simplest form the Salvo Model allows some very remarkable conclusions to be drawn when considering the present state of what Captain Wayne Hughes defined as a *Missile Age.*[17]

The Probability Factor

War, by definition, is probabilistic in nature and probabilities are a crucial element of military analysis since, as is the case for peaceful, everyday life; humanity is constantly engaged in risk assessment. Risk is a probability, also known by the lay public as "the odds," and we all are in constant, even if imperceptible, risk-assessing mode on a daily basis. While driving on the highway we constantly assess our risks, whether of getting into a major pileup, or of being stopped by a Highway Patrol for speeding. Throughout our lives, in general, we face a huge, ever-unfolding sequence of risks, which entail assessment of the probabilities of failures or successes, depending on one's point of view. Everyone does this risk assessment, even those people who never heard of Probability Theory or do not know even basic math, let alone the difference between deterministic and stochastic processes.

But if calculating or perceiving the risks of being hit by a car while crossing the street is very important for individuals, having a good idea of the risks involved in conducting warfare on a large, state-to-state, scale becomes a task of a vast importance to the entire nation, state and civilization. Military history has many examples illustrating how incorrect or successful risk assessment by military leaders has had a profound effect on the outcome not only of a single battle but on the outcome of the war itself and the further fate of the combatants. The Soviet STAVKA's protracted calculations and elaborations based on less than fully certain data prior to the Wehrmacht's unleashing its Operation Citadel in July 1943 around Kursk, provide a good example of risk assessment. Soviet defenses were preparing for the ultimate defeat of the Blitzkrieg in what amounted to the greatest armor clash in history.[18] A key to the Red Army success was the correct identification of the most probable targets for the Wehrmacht attack, later confirmed through intelligence, as well as the correct choice of counter-offensive once this strategic defense had blunted the initial Wehrmacht blows. This sequence of correct assessments and consequent planning led to victory in a key battle of WW II.[19]

But before any modern military commander, or analyst, begins to offer risk assessments, i.e. calculates the probabilities of failure or success of large operations, they must first have gone to what amounts to the "grammar school" of operational research related to probabilities. There is no understanding warfare without knowing what kind of probabilities are involved. Calculating the required force for accomplishing combat missions is one of the most important military tasks. For a military professional the same as for a serious statesman trying to make a well thought-out strategic decision, success is measured by the criterion of effectiveness i.e. the probability of success. The higher the probability of success, or effectiveness, the better the decision. It would be really unwise for a military leader to accept to go into battle under circumstances in which he, and his troops, would have less than good chances of winning unless they were forced to face the highest combat and moral challenge—a fight to death.

What, then, indicates a good chance of success? Military professionals like the chances or probabilities of any factors —from hitting the target, to detection of target, to winning the battle—to be as high as possible, preferably above 90%, or P=0.9 and higher. Consider this simple scenario of a tank engaging a terrorist target (a dugout in a rocky desert) while starting moving toward it from a distance equal to the maximum range of the tank's gun at night, shooting three shots. They would want to know what will be the effectiveness, expressed as a probability of the dugout destruction P_k, from three shots while on the move.

Some initial conditions for this scenario should be given. Let us assume that we know that on a number of both training and actual combat occasions, the tank and its crew recorded the following results:

The probability of hitting the target from the first shot $P_1 = 0.65$, from the second $P_2 = 0.72$ and from the third $P_3 = 0.87$. The weighted average, also known as mathematical expectation ω, of the number of shells required to destroy a target such a dugout, is around $\omega = 1.3$ shells. Pay attention to the fact that with each shot, because those shots are dependent events, as tank gets closer to the target and adjusts with each next shot, the probability of a hit grows. Here is the formula for the probability of a kill (or destruction) of a terrorists' dugout:

$$P_k = 1 - (1 - \tfrac{P_1}{\omega})(1 - \tfrac{P_2}{\omega})(1 - \tfrac{P_3}{\omega})$$

We can now plug in our numbers and see if our tank is effective enough to be sent into the battle:

$$P_k = 1 - (1 - \tfrac{0.65}{1.3})(1 - \tfrac{0.72}{1.3})(1 - \tfrac{0.87}{1.3}) =$$
$$= 1 - (1 - 0.5)(1 - 0.55)(1 - 0.67) = 1 - 0.5 \times 0.45 \times 0.33 = 1 - 0.07425 =$$
$$= 0.92575 \text{ or } 92.58\%$$

This is not a bad probability for the effectiveness of the tank and its crew, but still we can improve on this both theoretically and practically by:

1. Conducting more training for the crew, especially for the first shot;

2. Improving the night vision and ballistic computer of the tank;

3. Improving effectiveness of the tank's ammo against a variety of targets, including against dugouts.

Some other measures can also be implemented, but even this simple example gives a slight insight in how even basic operations are planned by competent officers and staffs. After all, both training and, especially, combat experiences and the correlates they provide, are crucial for development of both technology and tactics. From here we can easily calculate what would happen if a technologically advanced tank with a very well trained crew and new, highly efficient ammo with ω=1.1 had entered the fray, which had respective probabilities of 0.85, 0.92 and 0.95 for its three shots—here we would be looking at effectiveness of 99%. In fact, such a combination of new technology, involving first look, first shot, and first kill is nothing new, and such a combination will do, in its first two shots (94.7%), still better than our tank and crew in the original example with three shots.

Obviously, these are not the only combat tasks which probabilities allow military professionals to accomplish. Here's another example with tanks. Consider a scenario where a tank commander, knowing that all tanks in his battalion have around the same probability of a hit on the first shot of around $P_1 = 0.52$ when attacking in full speed, needs to know how many tanks he has to dispatch to a location of the enemy's MLRS to prevent it from launching before being obliterated. Here the emphasis is on the probability of a hit on a first shot. If such a commander wants to reach a very high probability of a kill, $P_k = 0.97$, he will have to use the formula which is a simplified version of the formula we used above:

$$P_k = 1 - (1 - P_1)^n$$

The exponent in this formula is a number of tanks he will need. The solution is very simple. We plug in numbers we have:

$$0.97 = 1 - (1 - 0.52)^n$$
$$0.03 = 0.48^n$$

Logarithms of both sides lead to the simplest linear equation:

$$n = -3.51 / -0.73 \approx 4.8$$

So, the battalion commander will need to dispatch $4.8 \approx 5$ tanks to be able to accomplish his task with a very good probability of 0.97 or 97%.

As you can see, there are many ways of judging combat performance, as well as ways of seeing its improvement.

But how is all this related to Revolution in Military Affairs, military balance or geopolitical status? The answer is very simple—directly. The mathematics introduced in this chapter—and we have just barely scratched the surface—has a direct bearing on the calculation of the way military balance shifts, both regionally and globally.

Obviously, the enemy always has a say in a battle and war and no mathematical model can ever exactly predict the outcome, especially, in the military field where often morale and training may compensate for some—by far not all— technological and even tactical deficiencies. But in the modern war of technologically advanced opponents even the immensely important factors of morale and brilliant tactics may not be enough to offset some of the new technological realities. And even immense military budgets mean very little when we speak about the era of the *Real* Revolution in Military Affairs which came about with hypersonic weaponry and has completely redefined the way wars will be fought or prevented, the latter being a much better option than fighting.

Neither the authors of the quantitative model of geopolitical status nor even the most advanced Western thinkers, including a plethora of think-tanks, could ever openly admit that these assessments of actual combat capability provide such an amazing insight into the military balance which, in the end, when projected against the background of real economies, provide a real measure of the geopolitical status and weight of the nation. The general public, and especially the Western public, due to its gullibility and general lack of desire to deal with any numbers, can't conceive of what has been happening in the military field in the last decade.

On January 10, 2019, *The National Interest* magazine published an alarmist piece titled *The Air Force Has a Plan to Save Navy Warships from Missile Attacks*. In it, the author, citing the missile threat from the Russian *Zircon 3M22* hypersonic missile, mentioned some USAF research solicitation for floating radar allegedly able to provide "over-the-horizon" capability for the U.S. Navy's ships, thus supposedly giving them a "little more time to prepare" for incoming, allegedly Russian, anti-shipping missiles.[20] Here on display was a typical lack of understanding of the issue of modern anti-shipping—and not only of hypersonic—weapons, since the defining feature of the latter is the fact that they are indeed impossible to defend against by current and future anti-missile systems—even when they theoretically could be detected, which is in itself a major technological challenge. The primary "defense" against such systems currently lies in the hope that they will malfunction, thus failing to engage the target.

Unlike the Mach=10+ capable *Kinzhal* (*Kh-47M2*) which received much publicity in the West after Vladimir Putin's Address to Russia's Federal Assembly on March 1, 2018, the *3M22 Zircon* remained somewhat of a mystery and in the shadow of its longer-range aeroballistic relative.

Yet, in Vladimir Putin's address to the Federal Assembly in February 2019, he himself disclosed some key data on Zircon, stating that the latter missile is capable of Mach=9 and ranges in excess of 1,000 kilometers.[21] Together with the *Kinzhal,* the deployment of the *Zircon* and its lighter version, designed also for the now well recognized small missile ships of *Karakurt* and *Buyan* (*Tornado*) classes, re-writes naval warfare completely on a scale comparable in its effect to the introduction of steam-powered ironclads into warfare that was previously defined by wooden sail ships and muzzle loaded cannons. This comparison, however, may still be insufficient since hypersonic anti-shipping missiles solve for the foreseeable future the most acute problem of naval warfare—the problem of a leaker or leakage, that is, of the enemy missiles "leaking through" fleets' defenses and hitting their targets.[22] It has already become patently clear, with the *Kinzhal* alone being in its IOC (Initial Operational Capability) in early 2018, that the Russian littoral and close sea zone was completely closed to any combination of naval forces trying to launch their missiles at Russia from the sea. But while the *Kinzhal* is an air weapon carried by the specially equipped *MiG-31K* and, in the nearest future, by modernized *TU-22M3M* bombers, the *Zircon* will become a mainstay of what today amounts to reborn Naval Missile Carrying Aviation (MRA), plus it can be launched from the surface and from underwater, gravely complicating the already almost impossible task of defending against even a salvo of 2 *Kinzhals.* It mattered above all, that even the mathematics making the case for the defenders wasn't there.

Thus *The National Interest's* desperate grasping at straws cannot obscure the simple fact that a salvo of 2, let alone 4 or 6 hypersonic missiles, couldn't be stopped by any U.S. or anyone else's weapon system. Stopping even a single *Zircon* with grossly inflated intercept capabilities is a monumental task for the U.S. Navy's latest versions of anti-missile systems. Highly speculative numbers were circulating in a Russian segment of the internet regarding the probability of intercepting such a weapon by the latest and prospective U.S. systems. They ranged from 0.05 to 0.1.[23] But even if one would consider these figures highly unlikely—in terms of them being too high!—the possibility of the intercept of a single *3M22 Zircon* by an Aegis platform such as latest *Arleigh Burke-class* DDG of Flight III variety, expressed as $P_{intercept} = 0.2$ for each Standard missile, one is still left struggling to find a realistic number and launch pattern of the SM-6, or any other defensive missile on such an occasion. Even basic calculations for good probability kill of $P_{kill} = 0.9$ for a single *Zircon* produces a grim picture for a defender:

$$0.90 = 1 - (1 - 0.2)^n$$
$$0.1 = 0.8^n$$
$$ln0.1 = nln0.8$$
$$n = -2.3 / -0.22 \approx 10.45$$

In other words, per this highly inflated intercept probability by a single defensive missile, it should take 10-11 missiles to intercept a single *Zircon*. It is, however, most likely that the real probabilities of intercept by a single defensive missile are, indeed, per the above-mentioned Russian speculation, hovering around 0.1 since, if to distill all the dramatic advantages *Zircon* provides even for a single attacker, it is impossible to ignore the fact that no U.S. Navy defensive missile can simply fly with the speeds of Mach=9 unless it is a ballistic interceptor such as the SM-3 missile, which is not designed to deal with a threat like the *Zircon*. In this case, the equation will look like this:

$$0.1 = 0.9^n$$
$$ln0.1 = nln0.9$$
$$n = -2.3 / -0.11 \approx 20.9$$

Theoretically, one will need 21 defensive missiles to stop a single Zircon, which is beyond the launch capabilities of the Aegis ships serving as escorts in the U.S. Navy's most important combat formation—the Carrier Battle Group.

Obviously, the picture changes more dramatically still, once one considers what a 4-missile salvo of such a weapon as the *Zircon* will look like. Addressing it requires, as you might have guessed already, a somewhat different formula yet again.[24] When launched from submarines, such as a group of two, one must use a formula which accounts for a distributed salvo, which complicates matters even more for the defending side, including this terrifying physical fact: missiles such as the *Kinzhal* or *Zirkon,* apart from the explosives carried onboard, possess on a terminal approach an immense kinetic energy which varies directly as a square of an already blistering speed and which alone would be sufficient for a single missile to destroy a target the size of a *Ticonderoga-class* cruiser or *Arleigh Burke-class* destroyer, thus providing these missiles with a crucial $\omega=1$ or near one for large surface combatants. These are very economical weapons. One can only speculate how many of these missiles it might take to disable a single U.S. Navy nuclear powered carrier. Removal of the Aegis-equipped escorts would seem to be the logical approach to operations against the U.S. Navy's carrier battle groups in the remote sea zones, where the very long ranges of both the *Kinzhal* and *Zircon* make the carriers of these weapons invulnerable to defensive interception operations by the carrier air-wing.

Thus Admiral Turner's strategic truism—"It isn't the number of keels, or size of ships that count. It is the capacity to do what might be decisive in some particular situation"—finds its empirical confirmation, when speaking about modern warfare. The large, imposing, and enormously expensive ships constituting the carrier battle groups are simply defenseless against the emergence today of revolutionary new weapons. If a single salvo of several *3M22 Zircons,* whose combined costs range somewhere around a few tens of millions of dollars, can decimate tens of billions of dollars' worth of hardware, and with it deal a strategic blow whose actual monetary value is even higher, reaching trillions of dollars' worth of trade, prestige, investment and other elements of what used to constitute the myth of American power, one must ask the question—how much is the size of the military budget, or expenditures M1 from a Status Model, really worth when large portions of it would simply be wiped out in a real war or even a simple exchange, without even having launched a single mission?

The answer is obvious—military expenditure is a worthless equivalency, good only for propaganda purposes. It cannot be applied to any calculations which ignore the serious operational and strategic ramifications of the proverbial bang for a buck. In real geopolitics it matters only what a weapon system can do and how it is deployed, not how much it is worth, which these days is measured in grossly inflated currency anyway.

CHAPTER 4

The Revolution in Military Affairs: Two Different Views

The term "Revolution in Military Affairs" (RMA) has been around for a long time. One observer described this phenomenon in the following terms:

> The revolution in military affairs is based primarily on the impact made by the advancement of technologies in the field of information technology, sensors, computing and telecommunications, and the modern military. The concept is defined in the Annual Report to Congress as: A Revolution in Military Affairs (RMA) occurs when a nation's military seizes an opportunity to transform its strategy, military doctrine, training, education, organization, equipment, operations, and tactics to achieve decisive military results in fundamentally new ways.[1]

Such a description became en vogue in the West, unsurprisingly, after the ultimate defeat of Saddam Hussein's Army in the First Gulf War. It was introduced in the United States by Andrew Marshall, the head of Net Assessment in the Pentagon.[2] But the term RMA didn't start with its present form. RMA was, initially, MTR (Military-Technological Revolution), introduced by Soviet military theoreticians in the 1970s. They identified three distinct MTRs in the twentieth century as follows:

1. The advent of motorization, the airplane, and chemical weapons during the First World War. With this MTR's maturation unfolded in WW II through the Blitzkrieg based on Panzer divisions (a tank brigade with four battalions, a motorized infantry brigade with four rifle battalions, an artillery regiment, and reconnaissance, antitank, and engineer battalions and service units), strategic bombardment as epitomized by the Anglo-American Combined Bomber Offensive against Germany, and the displacement of battleships by aircraft carriers in naval warfare.

2. The development of ballistic missiles and atomic weapons at the end of World War II, with this second MTR's maturation in 1970s with the USSR and the United States reaching a parity in nuclear weapons.[3]

3. The third MTR came about with the advent of High Precision/Precision Guided Munitions (PGMs), and Stand-off munitions, which may be launched at a distance sufficient to allow attacking personnel to evade defensive return fire from the target area. These inevitably required new sensors and processing technologies (computers).

Or, as another observer, Andrew F. Krepinevich, noted:

What is a military revolution? It is what occurs when the application of new technologies into a significant number of military systems combines with innovative operational concepts and organizational adaptation in a way that fundamentally alters the character and conduct of conflict. It does so by producing a dramatic increase—often an order of magnitude or greater—in the combat potential and military effectiveness of armed forces. Military revolutions comprise four elements: technological change, systems development, operational innovation, and organizational adaptation.[4]

There certainly were and still are sceptics both in regard to the validity of seemingly astonishing results obtained in the First Gulf War and in the supposedly massive institutional overhaul which the Third MTR encompassed. However, by the time the euphoria from the swift and overwhelming defeat of the third rate Iraqi Army subsided somewhat, and especially after both American and NATO operations in Iraq and Afghanistan ran into trouble, more sober and reflective voices started to be heard. While there was very little doubt that High Precision Weapons and processing power with sensors required for their use became the mainstay and thus could legitimately be termed a revolutionary development, one fact remained unchanged. It was noted by Center for Strategic and Budgetary Assessments in 2010:

Unquestionably the U.S. military has come a long way in embracing non-nuclear guided munitions since 1991. But like the German campaign in Poland in September 1939, the conflicts the U.S. military has fought in Afghanistan and Iraq have not been against major adversaries with comparable military capabilities. Against the Taliban, the Iraqi army, al Qaeda terrorists, Sunni and Shia insurgents, and various jihadist fighters from Iran and elsewhere in the Arab world, the increasing use of guided munitions by American forces has been less about new ways of fighting than about improving the efficiency and effectiveness of long-standing ways of fighting by traditional U.S. military organizations. U.S. progress in embracing the revolution in military affairs centered on precision-strike has to be assessed relative to capable adversaries with their own precision-strike capabilities, not relative to opponents with third-rate military capabilities.[5]

It was a late, however still important, admission which heeded, finally, the warning which a group of American RMA researches issued in 1995 regarding overreliance on the military element of American national power, which on the surface seemed to validate itself so well in the First Gulf War.[6] The reality of the Third MTR, or what came to be known in the U.S. as the RMA, was and remains very complex because, as was pointed out, assessing such a revolution in the context of a supremely inferior opponent was not a good idea, which, inevitably, lead the West in general, and the United States in particular, to a dramatic failure not only in forecasting, with any degree of accuracy, the future of warfare but to a failure in perceiving the complex dynamics of the changing global military balance.

Of course, the RMA is primarily a technological revolution, but it is also an operational, strategic and doctrinal one. But no technological revolution in military affairs since the late 19th century has been possible without the resources of a highly economically and technologically developed nation-state. Thus the foundation of the RMA, or at least of what passes for RMA today, depends on the nature of the nation-state. This moves the discussion on this extremely important issue into the realm of politics or, in more specific terms—policy. Moreover, it is the province of realistic scientific, military and industrial policies, which can originate only within highly developed nations. Technologies which come into RMA are so complex and require such a massive financial, material and human investment that only few selected nations can afford to take part as true driving forces of such a revolution. As an example, one of the staples of the RMA—the number of the nations which can produce modern stand-off munitions, such as land-attack cruise missiles, also known as TLAMs—can be counted on the fingers of one hand. Only the United States, Russia, China and France have the wherewithal to develop and produce out of their own resources such types of stand-off weapons. There are also rumors that the ever secretive Israel has developed its own venerable *Popeye* missile into a true long-range stand-off TLAM.[7] Yet, in this short list, only two nations have the full ability to provide *global* satellite guidance to their cruise missiles by virtue of owning satellite navigation systems: the American *GPS* and the Russian *GLONASS*. Neither China's *BeiDou* nor the European *Galileo* are as yet fully global positioning systems.

It doesn't warrant much elaboration on the issue of military technology and one of its derivatives, military power, as only being a function of an advanced nation. Only highly developed advanced economies are capable of producing the range of weapons and other combat systems which drive such a revolution. That is not a theorem anymore, it is an axiom, or what generally could be termed a truism. Non-state actors or relatively weak nations can produce some military technology, such as small arms, some vehicles and even some small naval vessels, some fairly simple electronics can also be assembled, but that is the extent of their possible weapon systems' development. Egypt, as an example, produces, that is to say assembles from American-made kits, U.S. designed M-1 Abrams tanks for its own defense needs.[8] A NATO member, Netherlands, being a first world developed nation, does produce a large share of its military equipment domestically, but even this economically relatively large nation increasingly depends on the United States to provide for its most important needs in Air Defense or Air Force fields. Royal Netherlands Air Force (RNLAF), as an example, operates only American designed and kitted F-16 fighter jets, with the F-35 planned as a substitute for the F-16 fleet in the next decade.[9] The explanation for this fact is very simple—no matter how developed the economy and military-industrial complex of Netherlands are, Netherlands lacks both the size and the scientific potential to produce, out of its own resources, any very high end weapons system, such as combat aircraft or a long range air-defense system, let alone integrate it in a way which allows its most effective use against threats. This, certainly, is not the recipe for any kind of revolution even when the nation operates seemingly very advanced weapons systems.

Mere operation, or even production, of some Precision Guided Munitions (PGMs) is also not in any way an indicator of a revolution. True revolution starts when all those weapon systems and sensors are integrated in such a way that their potential could be used to the full extent to achieve the objective which Clausewitz defined as compelling the enemy to do our will.[10] Those systems only become major drivers of RMA when several key conditions are met. It goes without saying that fulfilling those conditions is immensely expensive and beyond the reach of most nations. The requirements for drawing the conclusion that a Revolution in Military Affairs is real and not just a figment of the imagination must include several important milestones, as follows.

Net-Centric Warfare

There is no unanimity on the origin of the Net-Centric Warfare concept, albeit the term itself was coined by the late Admiral Cebrowski in his and John Garstka's 1998 article titled "Network-Centric Warfare—Its Origin and Future."[11] The term itself is very descriptive once one begins to consider what warfare really is about. Already in ancient times, when the first spear was thrown at a wild animal by a primitive human hunter, several factors determined a successful kill. Those factors were:

- A successful search, detection, tracking and location of an animal. The targeting process of modern weapon systems are a very remote relative of hunters' ability to move in for the kill.
- The ability to communicate with other hunters in a group while tracking the animal—a recognizable process of networking, involving voice and gesture communications.
- Reaching the final moment before a throw of the spear, or spears, a remote relative of modern firing solution. Here, calculations were done in hunters' brains without them being aware of whatever complex mathematics, physics and geometry might have been involved. Today we do know and we know how to calculate.
- Finally, the throw itself or, what is commonly known today as a salvo.

In general, warfare is about knowing where your target or targets are, what they are doing, and the ability to develop a firing solution. It goes without saying that such information, or as Norman Friedman defines it—*a picture-centric warfare*—is best obtained by more than one friendly and connected observer, thus creating a more reliable picture of the behavior of the target or targets.[12] Indeed, if doing a simple forensic experiment with a steamboat underway on the lake completely cloaked by the fog and whistling, a single observer on the shore would get a very approximate direction to the boat from the sound of this boat's whistle, but this observer's attempts to estimate distance to such a boat, however roughly, will be all for naught. The maximum such an observer will be able to do is to ascertain whether the boat is far or close, at best. This is not a very good estimate of boat's position. The addition of the second observer, however, granted that such an observer is removed sufficiently far from the first one along lake's shore, changes the picture quite dramatically.

It doesn't even require the use of range, grossly inaccurate as it is, and limits observations to only two direction obtained by our observers. What used to be a very approximate direction, or rather range of directions, to the boat from one observer, becomes "multiplied" by two when the second observer is involved and both observers can communicate and compare records. In reality they will superimpose their records for each given, time-coordinated moment of observation (hearing) of the boat's whistle. This immediately places the steamboat in a very specific area. For war this makes all the difference because it gives targeting, under the conditions of our example—very inaccurate but targeting nonetheless. In order to avoid complicated explanations of why the area (see figure) with the steam boat in it will be, in reality, an ellipse obtained by the means of fusion of two measurements by our observers, we will operate with a rather unremarkable quadrangle.

Targeting in modern war is not just a question of direction and range to the target, it also includes, granted the capability of modern weapon systems, geographic coordinates, which could be easily developed from the shooter's own position's direction and range to the target, and vice-versa. Of course in our steamboat example such an imprecise targeting, which gives only the area, is not good enough for shooting any kind of unguided projectile at the steamboat. With modern systems, such as an anti-shipping missile (ASM), however, shooting into the area is a normal procedure since modern ASM's targeting and homing systems, such as active radar seekers, allow for a refined search and lock onto target. But as the illustration shows, even such grossly inaccurate observations by two people on the shores of the lake can produce a very rudimentary targeting for a modern weapon by placing the target inside some area—in our case quadrangle ABCD.

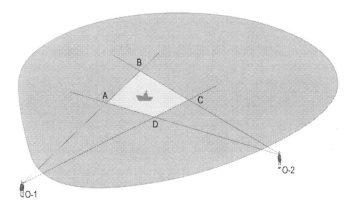

The method of what amounts to position fix by two bearings (ranges) has been known to navigation for centuries now. In laymen's lingo this method is known as a "triangulation" and this exactly what is in the foundation of positioning, be that oneself or the target in case of the network, together with other fairly basic methods. Here, we have deliberately chosen a very primitive scenario which does not really account for the capabilities and sophistication of modern systems such as radar, which allow the detection and tracking of targets with high accuracy based on only two parameters: bearing (azimuth) and range, with third parameter of angle of elevation (or depression) adding in case of air or air-defense operations.

We have provided this basic representation of the building blocks of the network, to demonstrate that the most important part of a combat network is not just the ability to make reliable observations, but the ability to communicate those observations into a larger picture of the events assembled on a higher tactical and operational levels. In other words— there is no network where there is no communications and even that is not enough. The first visual acquaintance with representations of net-centricity happened for the lay public with the release in 1986 of James Cameron's sci-fi action horror masterpiece *Aliens*. As might well have been appreciated by lay military strategists, Lieutenant Gorman was portrayed battle-managing a squad of his Colonial Marines from an armored personnel carrier using electronic and each marine's camera feed, allowing him to have a good situational and tactical awareness—until a surprise attack from alien vultures, that is. Cameron's prophetic vision, however, could not account for a dramatic increase of processing power and miniaturization of electronic devices in the 1990s and what that could bring to the tactical and operational level. It brought a lot.

In their seminal *Network Centric Warfare: Developing and Leveraging Information Superiority,* Garstka, Alberts and Stein elaborate extensively on one of the pillars of net-centric warfare concept—*Metcalfe's Law,* which states that the value of the network is measured in the number of potential informational interactions between similar nodes, or fax machines, as Law suggests, or, for that matter, soldiers or the aircraft or ships.[13] The larger the number of nodes, the greater the value of the network. Metcalfe's Law for a number n of possible informational interaction states that such a value is calculated by a simple formula of a simplex communication:

$$\frac{n(n+1)}{2}$$

In warfare, where informational interactions involve in very many cases duplex, that is, two nodes capable of "talking" back and forth to each other simultaneously, not a simplex method of communication, which allows the transmission of only one signal at a time, the value of such networks is calculated by even simpler formula:

$$n(n+1) = n^2 + n$$

Thus, for a network of 5 nodes (say 5 Colonial Marines) capable in theory to interact with each other simultaneously, the number of interactions will be potential interactions. For still larger networks this number approaches n^2. Extrapolating, the value of interactions between 1000 nodes thus equals one million. Of course, real life and real warfare do not work like this. They impose dramatic limitations and also complicate matters dramatically. In the end, not all communications are equal, nor are all nodes. There is a huge difference between a front line infantry man reporting to his superior on radio about observing for a few seconds a salvo of cruise missiles flying over his head and the air defense complex and AWACS plane exchanging radar and visual information on the same cruise missile salvo. The infantry man can only give an approximate position and a very inaccurate estimate of the speed and elevation of such a salvo, while AWACS will be translating to the Air Defense complex by far more useful information about such missiles' real time 3D position, course and speed—the precise data required for the air defense complex to develop a firing solution in order to intercept the incoming cruise missiles. In such a scenario it is obvious that value of a node, or, if one wishes, a sensor in a form of an infantry man is not really high because it provides very inaccurate information that is fast becoming obsolete, while the informational interaction between AWACS and air defense complex is absolutely crucial. In other words, only proper organizations and protocols can give meaning to Metcalfe's Law in the combat network.

Now, imagine not one, but five long range and seven medium range air-defense complexes, three-four Unmanned Aerial Vehicles (UAV) and two AWACS planes engaged in using all of their radar and optronic systems and communicating with each other constantly—this kind of interaction undeniably produces a much better picture of a battlefield. It also provides good targeting information and permitting a much faster decision on the battle and target distribution between available weapons. Modern processing power makes this possible. Under ideal conditions, that is. The United States military, in the words of David Ignatius quoted by General Latiff, envisions this technology within what is known as Third Offset strategy as: "'Network enabled semi-autonomous technology,' which allows weapons to communicate with one another to find targets if communications or sensor links to human decision makers are destroyed."[14]

Such an idea is not a new one. The Soviet Navy realized similar principles in its premier anti-shipping missiles of the 1980s and 90s, *P-700 Granit* (NATO *SS-N-19 Shipwreck*), which were fully networked in the salvo, able to communicate with each other, and capable of completely autonomous operations, including targets' distribution within the salvo, and Electronic Counter-Countermeasures (ECCM), and they were fully shoot-and-forget weapons.[15] For the mid-1980s this was an extremely impressive and, in many senses, revolutionary capability which was due to an explosive development of data processing technologies. The range of *P-700* missiles which was around 600 kilometers (roughly 324 nautical miles) changed naval warfare dramatically, making the area of operation for platforms which carried such a missile complex—nuclear powered submarines of *Project 949A (NATO Oscar II)*—an astonishing 1,130,400 square kilometers—roughly two thirds of the territory of the State of Alaska, or more than twice the area of California.

Communication technologies allowed a dramatic expanding of the geography of the battle-space, which inevitably, to-day, became global and capable of generating synergy—one of the main benefits attributed to networked forces, be that ground, air or naval ones.[16]

Already then, by the 1980s, the issue of informational overload, which was inevitable in the case of the creation of a fully net-centric force, became a serious problem. The same held true for the issue of data (sensor) fusion which was required for a combat network operating both homogenous and heterogeneous sensors. Targets could be detected and tracked by variety of sensors—from radar, to acoustic, to magnetic, to Infra-Red optronic means—which would help to resolve uncertainties with target(s) position. Resolution of those uncertainties became absolutely crucial in the modern warfare world where low observability in all spectra is a prime commodity.

Sensor (Data) Fusion

Here we are going to use interchangeably Sensor and Data Fusion since there is no meaningful difference between the two—sensors provide data, which is later fused. Some people even offer a new acronym for this: MSDF—Multi Sensor Data Fusion. As was demonstrated in the illustration for the steamboat and two observers on the shore of the lake, both, while observing (i.e. measuring) the position of the boat produced an uncertainty—using a philosophical, as opposed to purely mathematical, definition (in order not to complicate matters too much)—have some issues with reliability and/or confidence in their sensors, their ears. Similarly, listening-based devices, or large acoustic sensors, or microphones, were used by artillery for sound-ranging and by air-defense for detection of incoming enemy aviation as early as WW I. Effectively, the primitive sonar itself is nothing more than a large collection of microphones, also known as hydrophones, which allow a fairly accurate measuring of direction and range to the target.

Yet, no matter how accurate one's sensor is, all of them, without exception have instrumental and other types of uncertainties which are best resolved (that is dramatically reduced) by networking and fusing data from them. And again, even the inaccurate position of the steamboat in our example is obtained by homogenous sensor fusion, the ears of our observers, or rather fusion of their two measurements of the direction (bearing) to the boat. This is a primitive example of sensor fusion; a more complex example of data fusion would be a track of a large vessel, tanker or aircraft carrier, which could be, as it was often done, created on the main display at the command post on land, by means of combining tracks from over-the-horizon land-based radar, the radar of the ship shadowing the vessel and acoustic track from a system similar to American SOSUS (Sound Surveillance System) or any other ocean surveillance system, to create a much better track for such a target. Today one may add into this mix long range UAVs and satellites. All those means are engaged with a simple mission in mind—to resolve uncertainty in precisely locating enemy targets.

Let's take this to an even more complex example, the *Russian S-400 Triumph (*NATO *SA-21 Growler)* one of the most capable weapon systems in the world, which integrates not only other air-defense complexes, such as *S-1 Pantsir (*NATO *SA-22 Greyhound)* but also is able to integrate its own organic detection systems with such low-frequency radar as *Nebo-SVU,* which allows it, by means of data fusion, to resolve uncertainties associated with detection, tracking and developing a firing solution against stealth aircraft. In fact, most Russian modern air defense complexes, including the S-300PMU, could serve as an exhibit A of the net-centric warfare and sensor fusion.[17]

The modern battlefield, which involves a myriad of informational interactions, becomes extremely informationally dense. In order to be able to sort out this gigantic flow of information and not get overwhelmed, a number of tools are used which allow both the analysis of events and keeping the system running. One of them is to encapsulate or subordinate some networks; obviously, for the head of strategic command and his staff, it is not imperative to be involved in the tactical network of some specific company, let alone platoon, albeit modern technology allows them to obtain feeds, if need be, from a single infantryman to be filed directly to highest command. But the tactical level networking is called tactical for a reason since it is limited to a tactical command level, which in most armed forces is the level of brigade or division, with the next level—the level of the army corps—being a tactical-operational level and thus operating a higher (or lower—depending on the point of view) network.

Another way to address the vast stream of data while fusing it is by means of a so-called *Kalman Filter,* which allows refined guesses (predictions) of the future observed parameters using existing evidence on the basis of what is called "statistical significance." Putting it very simply, a *Kalman Filter* permits a reliable estimate of the next parameter.[18] Such a filter is widely used in data fusion and is crucial in such fields as Electronic Counter-Countermeasures (ECCM). As was already stated, the simplest data fusion example is fixing the steamboat position by two separate bearings (directions). But one of the most down-to-earth and best comprehended cases of sensor fusion is the identification of anonymous communications based on the CDR (Call Detail Record) datasets of the mobile phone networks and geo-localized messages on the social networks, such as Facebook or Instagram.[19] In fact, similar techniques are used by police detectives who recreate the position of a suspect, or a victim, based on the cell-phone towers' pings and communicating with eye-witnesses.

The scenario for, say, repulsing the attack by an anti-shipping missiles salvo against surface ships will employ exactly the same networking and data fusion, which allows all ships in the group to sense, to exchange tracking data about, and to develop firing solutions against the attacking missiles. This capability is titled Cooperative Engagement Capability (CEC) in the United States and this is how the U.S. Navy defines it:

> Cooperative Engagement Capability (CEC) is a real-time sensor netting system that enables high quality situational awareness and integrated fire control capability. It is designed to enhance the anti-air warfare (AAW) capability of U.S. Navy ships, U.S. Navy aircraft and U.S. Marine Corps (USMC) Composite Tracking Network (CTN) units by the netting of geographically dispersed sensors to provide a single integrated air picture, thus enabling Integrated Fire Control to destroy increasingly capable threat cruise missiles and aircraft.[20]

It is a sensible solution and the ships of the group under attack will detect and track incoming missiles using both their radar and optronic sensors. Each ship then, while fusing its own data, will also do a fusion with the data from other ships in the group, thus obtaining much better missile tracks if that process had been limited to a single ship and its sensors. CEC provides for a greater situational awareness by presenting a single composite picture of the battlefield. It also increases combat stability, which is the ability to retain the capability to continue the fight under the impact of enemy forces by means of a more efficient use of defensive weapons. That is, of course, in theory and if everything works as planned, which is never the case in real life since a huge number of factors begins to affect operations.

For starters, the era of the subsonic anti-shipping missiles is over—the main type NATO navies will be facing are high supersonic, and violently maneuvering on the terminal approach, ASMs of the Russian *P-800 Onyx (Oniks)* variety or, by now globally famous ASMs of the *Kalibr-class, 3M54.* Moreover, the environment in which these missiles will be used in case of war will be characterized as a highly hostile Electronic Warfare environment. This is if we discount such massively important factors as weather and personnel training on the ships under attack. This, of course, brings forth the question of whether Net-centricity and Data Fusion are everything they were promised to be from the get go. No, they are not, which, however, in no way disparages the benefits they bring to the modern battlefield.

Net centricity is here to stay and it is an axiom. Every developed modern military today applies Net-centric warfare principles in their technological and operational approaches. In actual combat operations such as in the Donbass, NCW principles, based on Russia's C4ISR capabilities made available by the Russian military to numerically inferior armed forces of Donbass Republics (LDNR), were used to a devastating effect both at the Battles of Ilovaisk and Debaltsevo, when attacking the cumbersome Soviet-era Ukrainian Armed Forces military fashioned after the 1980s which was denied effective command and control, and use of their military both due to the very high mobility of rebel forces and to Russia's EW capabilities.[21] In the end, net centricity's operational effect had a crucial dependence on communications and communications can be suppressed or disabled altogether. Russia's foremost authority on NCW, Lieutenant Colonel Kondratiev of Russia's Academy of Military Sciences, while being a dedicated proponent of NCW, was forced to admit that NCW is "not a panacea" and problems do exist.[22] Related events experienced in the joint U.S.–South Korean Staff exercises in 2011, when DCGS (Distributed Common Ground System) malfunctioned and left U.S. Staff in a complete situational darkness, was a good reminder of the vulnerabilities even most advanced systems exhibit under some real war circumstances. Real war being the ability of a near peer or peer to disrupt the enemy's electronic systems.

Yet, as always is the case with any new technology or concept, some radical views on Net-centricity didn't fail to materialize. U.S. Marine Corps Lieutenant General Paul Van Riper, in his interview to PBS in 2004, was blunt:

> My experience has been that those who focus on the technology, the science, tend towards sloganeering. There's very little intellectual content to what they say, and they use slogans in place of this intellectual content. It does a great disservice to the American military, the American defense establishment. "Information dominance," "network-centric warfare," "focused logistics"—you could fill a book with all of these slogans. What I see are slogans masquerading as ideas. In a sense, they make war more antiseptic. They make it more like a machine. They don't understand it's a terrible, uncertain, chaotic, bloody business. So they can lead us the wrong way. They can cause people not to understand this terrible, terrible phenomenon.[23]

As late as 2017 some Russian specialists continued to warn about complexity and the vulnerability to suppression of combat networks based on the processing of heterogeneous information. Among several crucial vulnerabilities pointed out was the overestimation of human capacity to adequately process vast volumes of information, excessive information-al dependency of all parts of the network, and overall extreme complexity of the net-centric systems, among many others, not least of which is resorting to a COTS (Commercial off the Shelf) approach aimed at reducing extreme costs.[24] In the end, General Van Riper was the man who allegedly defeated the most advanced operational and technological concepts of the era in 2002 in a shocking—for proponents of RMA—military exercise, *Millennium Challenge 2002*. The very foundation of an American hi-tech vision of the warfare which was grounded in the assumption "that in the future the United States would have the real-time radar and sensor capabilities to eliminate them," turned out to be not well grounded in reality.[25] That one will have wonderful *CEC* and one's own sensors and weapons operating as intended, are not good assumptions when dealing with a serious opponent. In the end, as "low tech" victory of Van Riper over his net-worked opponents during the Millenium Challenge showed, tactical and operational acumen of leaders and ability to fight under the most restrictive conditions of proverbial *Fog of War* mattered and still matters a great deal.

This doesn't mean that principles of NCW are not valid. They are, but they are not a panacea on which all bets may be placed, as was stated by Lt. Colonel Kondratiev. Here one is forced to consider the necessary balance which must be found between net-centricity and what many proponents of NCW viewed as an outdated principles of platform-cen-tricity. Chief of Naval Operations Admiral Jay Johnson defined the process of increasing importance of net-centric-ity as *a fundamental shift from platform-centric warfare.*[26] Obviously, the idea that in real war, everything that was broadly defined as an information advantage due to the net-centricity does not deny in any way the importance of a single platform (which incidentally is one of the constituent parts of a network by definition) did not occur to most ardent supporters of NCW. The main question—what will a single ship, aircraft or platoon do under the most likely conditions when the network is down due to enemy's actions—seems to be not in the focus of current American strategic thought, at least one which is broadly represented by Pentagon and corporate top brass.

In fact, while networking is important for warfighting and it is here to stay, in the end success is all about what a specific platform, also known as a single shooter, and weapons it carries, can do in real war. It goes without saying that under the conditions of degraded combat networks, platforms will have to develop situational awareness on their own—they will have to get their very own picture of the battlefield and often act autonomously. The Soviet and present Russian Navy have experience in developing such solutions, despite Russia's presently engaging actively in networking of its Armed Forces. As an example older Soviet destroyers of the *Sovremenny-class* (Project 956) are armed with different versions of the *Mineral-ME* (NATO–*Band Stand*) radar system which, in its latest configurations, is capable of over-horizon detection ranges in active mode of up to 250 kilometers and in passive, up to 400 kilometers, while simultaneously exchanging data with up to 9 ships in group at a distance of 30 kilometers.[27] *Mineral-ME,* as well as many other similar systems capable of detecting and designating targets for their own ASM complexes, or exchanging such data with other sources, including aircraft, can hardly be called platform-centric, but this is exactly what well-known American naval analyst Norman Friedman called it.[28]

But the significance of *Mineral-ME* is not just its ability to be networked, which puts Friedman's statement into doubt; it is its ability to see and develop firing solutions for its *P-270 Moskit* (NATO–*SS-N-22 Sunburn*) ASMs at their very maximum range which is 240 kilometers in the latest versions of this deadly missile. In simpler language that means that *Mineral-ME* is able to detect a target, establish bearing and range to it, and track the target's movement while the salvo of *Moskits* is launched. Considering *Moskits*'blistering cruising speed of Mach=2.35 (2.35 speeds of sound) with it accelerating to almost Mach=3 at the terminal approach, it

Illustration credit: RosOboronExport

would take a salvo of several *Moskits* roughly 5-6 minutes to reach the target's location.[29]

A good idea of a single platform equipped with *Mineral-ME* or similar systems' ability to develop their own picture of a battlefield even without networking is well illustrated by calculating the area of a circle whose radius is three quarters of *Mineral-ME* in passive mode, that is, roughly 300 kilometers. Using a formula known from school to determine the area of the circle one can easily calculate that a single platform would be able to cover a circle of roughly 283,000 square kilometers area which easily translates, for comparison, into the area of the United Kingdom with the Kingdom of Netherlands' area added for good measure. Acting in a group of three ships—a network—such an area grows larger still. This is platform capability, from which one can hardly call, in the words of Admiral Jay Johnson, for a *fundamental shift*. Not only do the capabilities of a single platform still constitute the foundation on which the rest of the considerations are built, it is the single platform capability which matters, primarily in the case of a very real war when most benefits ascribed to NCW principles will be largely removed.

In other words, there is no factual *fundamental shift from* platform-centricity, especially against the background of a revolutionary development of missile systems which themselves behave as single platforms requiring only initial targeting data, geographic coordinates or bearing and range, to be able to reach the approximate area of a target and then using its own on-board means to conduct *final search*—in Russian it reads as *Dorazvedka or final refined search*—and acquire target for a final approach. The real revolution in military affairs starts with modern hypersonic fully shoot-and-forget weaponry whose capabilities trump completely any kind of net-centricity by virtue of those weapons being simply un-interceptible by any existent means. Enter Russia's latest missile, a hypersonic Mach=10 aero-ballistic *Kinzhal*. No existing anti-missile defense in the U.S. Navy is capable of shooting it down even in the case of the detection of this missile, which flies in a hot plasma cloud while maneuvering at the terminal approach to the target. *Kinzhal's* astonishing range of 2000 kilometers makes the carriers of such a missile, MiG-31K and TU-22M3M aircraft, invulnerable to the only defense a U.S. Carrier Battle Group, a main pillar of U.S. naval power, can mount—carrier fighter aircraft at their stations around CBG. Carrier aviation simply doesn't have the range.

A couple of MiG-31K with *Kinzhals* only needs a rough targeting data to launch their weapons after a Mach=2.5 dash to a drop point. *Kinzhal* can cover 2000 kilometers in roughly 10 minutes—hardly any meaningful time for an aircraft carrier, or any other ship—even granted they know the time of launch at them, a rather dubious assumption—to leave the area in which they will be acquired by *Kinzhal's* warhead.

That is a revolutionary capability and it is primarily platform-centric, once one considers that all modern anti-shipping and other cruise missiles are capable of conducting fine search, and dealing fairly well with uncertainties which appear because of the inaccuracies of the targeting, human mistakes and other factors constituting this proverbial fog of war—precisely the issue which Net Centric Warfare principles sought to address by means of leveraging the informational superiority. On March 1, 2018, in Vladimir Putin's address to Federal Assembly in which he unveiled some of Russia's new weaponry, including the *Kinzhal,* the real revolution in military affairs has arrived and this one changed completely the face of peer-to-peer warfare, competition and global power balance dramatically. We will assess the real effects of this revolution in the next chapters.

CHAPTER 5

The End of Invulnerability

In a conventional clash on the seas, be that on the high seas, in remote sea zones, or in a littoral of Russia, the U.S. Navy's surface fleet will simply not survive.[1] A two *Zircon* or *Kinzhal* missile salvo guarantees at least one leaker against any type of a surface target would get through, and would be sufficient to destroy a target of the modern destroyer size.[2] This is a radical departure from an earlier era's potential salvos by super-sonic missiles of *3M54* or *P-800 Onyx* (*Oniks*) variety which, while they are more complex and deploy more missies, would have required a significantly larger number of carriers, such as combination of *TU-22M3M,* surface ships and subs, needed to launch enough missiles to break through the anti-missile defenses of a carrier battle group. Both the *Kinzhal* and *Zircon* have changed all that. The ramifications of such a change are strategic and historic in nature. They allow, in Admiral Turner's words for a "capacity to do what might be decisive in some particular situation." Some "particular situation" in this case leads to an implosion of U.S. naval doctrine because its key assumption, the dramatic technological superiority of the U.S. Navy in an enemy's littoral, becomes entirely wrong.

This assumption has been wrong for quite some time. But this time around, new technical and operational properties of hypersonic weapons are such that they do provide a technological leap ahead which rewrites the warfare book radically—this is a definition of a revolution in military affairs. It is, of course, very premature to talk about complete obsolescence of modern surface fleets but it certainly spells doom for carrier-centric navies as fleets designed to fight for sea control against peers or near-peers. As a carrier-centric navy the U.S. Navy is not a force which can fight and win against Russia and China in their littorals. A number of U.S. top officials, including General John E. Hyten and the Government Accountability Office were explicit when stating "China and Russia are pursuing hypersonic weapons because their speed, altitude, and maneuverability may defeat most missile defense systems, and they may be used to improve long-range conventional and nuclear strike capabilities. There are no existing countermeasures."[3]

General Hyten went further, admitting to the U.S. Senate Armed Service Committee that the only defense against such weapons is a nuclear deterrent.[4] While Hyten was speaking primarily about strategic hypersonic glide vehicles such as Russia's *Avangard* capable of Mach=27 and its capacity for maneuvers which render anti-ballistic missile systems useless, it is clear that nominally anti-shipping missiles such as the *Zircon* or *Kinzhal* are also matters of grave concern, especially after *Kinzhal* successfully destroyed the land target the size of a passenger sedan in Syria from a distance of 1,000 kilometers in adverse weather conditions.[5] The implications of the *Kinzhal* precision land-attack capability cannot be overstated since that makes even NATO's hardened command and control facilities in Europe indefensible.

Zircon's claimed land-attack capabilities, however, were met with mixed reaction on part of some Russian analysts such as Captain 1st Rank (Ret.) Konstantin Sivkov who tried to contradict statements by Rear-Admiral (Ret.) Khmyrov— and that of Putin—that stressed that the *Zircon* is a strictly anti-shipping missile. It was a strange argument since anti-shipping missiles have been used to attack land targets on numerous occasions, from the SSGN of Oscar-II class striking a radio-contrast target at the range on Novaya Zemlya with its *SS-N-19* (*P-700 Granit*), while the land-based anti-shipping complex Bastion, armed with the *P-800 Onyx* missiles, was successfully used against ISIS targets in Syria.[6] However Rear-admiral Khmyrov does have a point—the unification of anti-shipping and land-attack functions for at least some missile complexes is not particularly new in principle for Russia which always had a secondary anti-shipping capability in most of its air-defense complexes. This was a road which Raytheon took in 2016 when testing the anti-air (anti-cruise missile) SM-6 in anti-shipping mode, allegedly sinking the retired *USS Reuben James* frigate.[7]

But if the *P-800 Onyx* or, even more so, the hypersonic *Kinzhal's* land attack test and combat experiences are any indicator, the *Zircon* definitely is capable of a secondary land-attack role and Khmyrov was correct to point out this weapon as capable of destroying coastal command and control centers and military installations with *Zircons* launched from the submarines or surface ships off the coasts of the United States.[8] The Western media did take note, and as usual missed the main message about the weapon itself that Vladimir Putin delivered to Federal Assembly on February 20, 2019. Some went into wildly inaccurate speculations, such as Charlie Gao's March 9th article in *The National Interest*.[9] Why a student of computer and political science would be afforded a say in a field in which he has no expertise other than "commenting" remains a complete mystery, one unfortunately symptomatic with the overall level of public military "expertise" and debate in the United States over the last decade which omits or obfuscates crucial technical, tactical and operational factors which should be professionally or at least competently discussed.

The *Zircon,* a weapon primarily but not exclusively designed to be carried by surface ships and submarines, represents a further development of a conventional threat against the U.S. proper—one of the weapons designed to fundamentally and forcefully change of the worldview of the United States elites, leaving nuclear weapons as a last-resort alternative. As one of the leading Russian Americanists, Dmitry Drobnitsky, commenting on the United States abandoning the INF Treaty and the U.S. delusion concerning its ability to security itself from retaliation, noted with a great deal of sarcasm: "United States abandoning the INF Treaty should not surprise anyone... They will continue to build their Anti-Ballistic Missile System. Maybe they will do it for eternity, but they will do it. And if they need to saturate space with weapons, they will do it."[10]

The introduction of hypersonic weapons surely pours some serious cold water on the American obsession with securing the North American continent from retaliatory strikes. If the introduction of the very long range sub-sonic *SLAM X-101* was an unpleasant surprise, since it opened a possibility of a massive conventional strike on land targets in North America, at least there was some formal argument in favor of an air defense which could intercept some of those missiles. But Russia's moving its hypersonic missiles close to the American shores is a complete game-changer.

An examination of simple geometry explains why. The area of the geometric figure formed by following a contour of the U.S. coasts in a distance of around 1000 kilometers into the oceans' expanse—providing a very rough estimate of the size of the area of the United States' East Coast from where submarines and surface ships armed with *Zircon* will be able to strike coastal areas with all command and control and military installation—is around 3,000,000 square kilometers, which is roughly the area of such a country as India.

In protecting this expanse, the first issue any military planner will seek to resolve is how to simply *detect Zircon* carriers, be that surface combatants (relatively easy) or submarines (much more difficult). The answer to this question—an intuitive solution of increasing numbers of heterogeneous force needed to detect and annihilate such carriers—is not as straightforward as it may appear. Of course, numbers do matter—the more the U.S. Navy's submarines, surface ships and aircraft of patrol aviation are involved in what is known as scouting or search operations, the greater is their probability of detecting (and destroying) enemy ships and submarines in case of war. But here is the catch: modern Russian submarines, such as the latest *Yasen-class* (*Project 885, NATO Graney/Severodvinsk-class*) SSGNs such as the class namesake or the new *Kazan,* an upgrade to *Project 885M* which will join the fleet in 2019, are quiet, while the other 5 hulls being built are extremely quiet.[11] Some American military analysts compare this class of Russian subs to the U.S. *Seawolf-class* SSNs in terms of quieting and other crucial characteristics, regarding them as one of the two quietest, if not the quietest, submarine classes in the world.[12]

Each *Yasen* was designed from the outset to carry latest and prospective cruise missiles, 32 of them. It would be highly imprudent to speculate on the complement of weapons each *Yasen* and the *Project 949A* (*Oscar II-class*) SSGNs, in the process of being upgraded, can carry, but it is clear that each sub will have enough firepower to launch an unstoppable salvo both at surface and land targets while being able to largely avoid all the old submarine retaliation problems known in professional circles as the *Flaming Datum* problem—a submarine's giving up its position after its torpedo or missile hits the enemy—because of the great ranges of its weapons. This problem is as old as the submarine as a platform, itself. Today, with the revolutionary development of acoustic and non-acoustic methods of submarine detection, the *Flaming Datum* problem as it was previously known, has changed dramatically. As at 2019:

1. Advanced submarines can detect each other's launches of either torpedoes or missiles over increased distances, sometimes ranging in hundreds of kilometers with accuracies affording a first and fairly precise estimation of its maneuvering elements (course, speed, depth) of a submarine;

2. Ranges of weapons. As development of such weapons as the *P-700 Granit* (*SS-N-19 Shipwreck*) missile complex demonstrated, once the range of the missile, 500+ kilometers for *Granit,* became comparable to the ranges of carrier aviation, the tactics changed.[13] The main concern for a missile firing submarine, in addition to their traditional danger from Patrol Aviation, shifted squarely to the danger of enemy submarines serving in an Anti-Submarine Warfare (ASW) role. Surface ASW forces became an important but now secondary threat, by the virtue of the increased distances of missile launch by submarine, because such distances mitigated greatly the main ASW asset of surface combatants—their ASW helicopters.

In other words, the main submarine strike weapon for surface targets became the anti-shipping missile, not the torpedo, which now is reserved, together with anti-submarine rockets such as *Shkval,* or *RPK-7 Veter* (*SS-N-16 Stallion*), primarily for submarine-to-submarine encounters.

Even before *Granit,* not to speak of *Zircon,* the problem of *Flaming Datum* still assuming that the launch could be detected by acoustic or other means, was, in layman's lingo, pushing it. Even if one could assume that the surface group could detect and survive relatively intact the first salvo of *Granit* launched from the distance of 350 kilometers, and launch its own ASW helicopters, a crucial issue for any search conducted as a consequence of *Flaming Datum* remained—the Delay Time (τ-Tau) for the helicopter to arrive at the datum (the launch point).[14] It was one thing to arrive at a datum which was 30-40 or even 50 kilometers away—the high speed of the helicopter, even with added delay time for going into combat station, starting the engines and lift off, was still allowing a sensible amount of time for a random search in the circle whose radius was expanding at the speed of the enemy submarine trying to flee. Even a 50-kilometer range could be covered by a MH-60R Seahawk ASW helicopter in under 20 minutes. However, at the 350-kilometer range the Seahawk would have reached the datum in about an hour and a half, at the very edge of its effective range and required time on station. It would then have been forced to conduct a search in a much wider circle, considering the launching submarine's contact breaking-off speed of about 10 knots (roughly 18.5 kilometers per hour), leading to a search area of around 2,500 square kilometers. After that it is up to the Seahawks' sensors, primarily dipping sonar and sonobuoys, to detect the submarine. What about a salvo launch range of 500 kilometers, then? This drops effectiveness of the search dramatically since it allows the submarine almost 2.5 hours to escape, while greatly reducing the time of the helicopter on station, plus presenting it with the necessity to search an area of roughly 6,700 square kilometers. It is not difficult to grasp that launches of missiles from the ranges of 800 kilometers and further make any deployment of present and prospective ASW helicopters completely impractical since they will not even make it to the datum due to lack of fuel.

This trend was already evident in 1980s. Today it is not just a trend—it represents a complete change in the nature of warfare. Even the most elaborate calculations and models can not obscure the rather grim fact that even if some ASW assets make it to the datum, will those helicopters have any ships left to return to? Even if we assume that the *Zircon* doesn't fly at hypersonic speed all the time but accelerates only to Mach=9 while entering the anti-missile zone of the surface force, it becomes patently clear that flying at M=4 for 600 kilometers it would make it to the terminal acceleration zone in roughly 8 minutes, while covering the terminal 200-300 kilometers in roughly a minute and a half. Under ten minutes, in this instance. With the *Zircon* slated to become fully operational and be deployed to a variety of platforms in 2023, it becomes quite clear that will be not just another huge leap in already massive warfare revolution in the ocean, but it will be further erosion of the American, largely self-proclaimed, hegemony in the environment where only a decade ago she had an advantage—naval warfare.[15]

The reason for such a development is an incessant pursuit of greater speeds and longer ranges of main strike weapons on the seas, ground and in the air—missiles. Even before the *Zircon* becoming a very tangible reality and the *Kinzhal* becoming fully operational, the M=2.5 + capable *P-800 Onyx* (*SS-N-26 Strobile*) was in service for some years. *Onyx's* 600+ kilometer range, similar to the range of the M=2.9 capable *3M54 Kalibr* anti-shipping missile, make both of these weapons capable of stretching an opponent's ASW capabilities to the very limit when launched at maximum range or near it.[16] Modern space based and distributed surface and underwater platforms and sensors do allow targeting for such types of launches, while reducing the launch time of several missiles to a few seconds. As the launch of the six-*Kalibr*-missile salvo by a newest Russian Navy's SSK at the ISIS targets in Deir ez-Zor in Syria on October 5, 2017 demonstrated, it took roughly 15 seconds for all 6 missiles to get airborne.[17] The salvo of only six high supersonic, maneuvering and networked sea-skimming anti-shipping missiles leaves very few chances for modern air-defense to react and provide for even semi-effective response to such a salvo which is configured to guarantee one or more leakers.

The situation, moreover, is not helped by the fact that the modern Russian Navy went back to the posture which the Soviet Navy exercised, maintaining a large fleet of bombers, known as MRA (Naval Missile Carrying Aviation), designed specifically for strike missions at surface targets. Unlike this force of the 1970s or 1980s, however, the new and upgraded Russian bombers carry missiles which are a radical improvement over the missiles of the 1980s. As the United States Naval Institute noted in 2019—*The Russian Air Force's bomber fleet is back in the antiship strike business.*[18] In this case, with or without the *Zircon* being operational, upgraded TU-22M3 and *TU-22M3M Backfire* bombers already bring near or full hypersonic capability deep into the ocean zone through both the operational 1000-kilometer range M=4+ capable *Kh-32* missile and the 2000-kilometer range M=10 capable *Kinzhal*.[19] In case of an actual war, their launches will happen beyond the ranges of retaliatory carrier aviation, thus reducing Carrier Battle Groups to a collection of targets of various sizes and prestige.

Some in the United States Navy, at least, are not oblivious to the developing situation. As Dr. Schneider warns:

> The U.S. Navy probably will face an antiship threat from the Backfire for another 20 years. The antisurface strike missiles we currently know about will not be the end of Russian development in this warfare area. Before the Backfire is retired and replaced by the Pak DA heavy stealth bomber, even more advanced missiles, including those with greater stealth and hypersonic speeds, will be fielded.[20]

While calls from different quarters of U.S. defense establishment to develop effective counters to this threat are
only natural, it is highly unlikely that such practical, that is,
effective, solutions will be found any time soon. Trying to
reshuffle the existing legacy, even of the most advanced systems and the tactics of their use, provides no solution which,
undeniably, will be found only in the field of new physical
principles incorporated into the future weapons systems.

This reality, however, is very slow to dawn on most U.S.
policy-makers who, for the most part, lack the necessary tool-
kit for grasping the unfolding geostrategic reality in which
the real revolution in military affairs—not least through a
massive deployment of operational-tactical and strategic
systems, such as the M=27 capable *Avangard* system—has
dramatically degraded the always inflated American military
capabilities and continues to redefine U.S. geopolitical status away from its self-declared hegemony. Moreover, such
weapons ensure a *guaranteed retaliation* on the U.S. proper
in not just its nuclear variants but now most significantly in
conventional warfare. Even the existing Russian, and to a
lesser degree the Chinese, nuclear deterrents are capable of
overcoming the existing U.S. anti-ballistic missile systems
and destroying the United States. But being able to strike
conventionally has its own great strategic benefits since it
adds another possible conventional phase short of an escalation towards the nuclear threshold in case of war. This phase
matters. Even despite its declaration concerning increasing
U.S. reliance on nuclear weapons in its 2018 NPR (Nuclear
Posture Review), it is clear that if the parties to a conflict
are rational actors, they would try to avoid nuclear confrontation up to the very last, as recent clashes between India
and Pakistan demonstrated—despite militant rhetoric and
conventional clashes, both nuclear states in the end decided
to de-escalate. In other words, they behaved, in the end, as

rational actors. But the contemporary United States is not a rational actor, not least due to American elites' unreasonable, indeed paranoid, fear that the United States proper could be attacked. But the recognition of a crucial distinction between a nuclear, even if limited, strike on the U.S. proper and a conventional one is in order.

It was the late Richard Pipes who recognized a defining feature of American attitudes towards war when he noted that:

> Extreme reliance on a technological superiority, characteristic of U.S. warfare, is the obverse side of America's extreme sensitivity to its own casualties; so is indifference to the casualties inflicted on the enemy.[21]

Considering Americans' profoundly traumatic reaction to the attack of 911, which, despite its spectacularly gruesome visuals, was not significant militarily, unlike the attack on Pearl Harbor where a large portion of the U.S. Pacific Fleet was either sunk or damaged, with 2,403 killed, most of them U.S. servicemen, the whole notion of American soil being attacked not by some terrorists utilizing civilian aircraft or by a nuclear holocaust, but rather by conventional weapons, is simply beyond the emotional grasp of most Americans. The truth, however, is very simple—the logic behind the notion of conventional strikes on U.S. soil is that of counter-force, not counter-value. Modern conventional stand-off precision weapons can have an impact equaling or surpassing that of nuclear weapons—and without nuclear fallout. It is well known fact that the Pentagon's now removed hot dog stand and its new dining iteration in the middle of the Pentagon building's geometric center is called Café Ground Zero for a simple reason—rumor had it that the USSR had at least two missiles aimed at the Pentagon's courtyard.[22]

It doesn't take an academician to have a rough understanding of what a single megaton-level yield MIRV could do, not just to the Pentagon, to say nothing of its famous diner, but also to its surroundings in Arlington County and District of Columbia. No matter the ever-increasing accuracy of nuclear warheads, a strike on Pentagon, however nominally a counter-force, would create massive civilian casualties and catastrophic destruction. That is, until the effectiveness and precision of hypersonic weapons reached the plateau which does allow us to talk about real counter-force, with long range hypersonic weapons having accuracy in meters and being, indeed, surgical by being able to limit the destruction to a designated target and its very immediate vicinity only. This is a new paradigm facing the United States, which for decades was used to thinking about itself as the only power capable of precision conventional strikes, while simultaneously trying to over-represent the Gulf War to influence the nuclear posture of Russia in the 1990s and 2000s—despite well documented arguments on the Russian side that such a war could not be used as a standard against which to judge the nature of modern war.[23] It was a correct assessment on the Russian side, especially against given the grossly uninformed American position that Russia didn't have stand-off precision weapons despite the fact that the USSR/Russia was already leading the United States in guided missiles technologies by way of a variety of naval anti-shipping missiles which, by definition, were stand-off precision weapons.

While hypersonic weapons are capable of delivering a nuclear payload to the target it is their conventional properties which create a strategic ambiguity of sorts which, in this case, favors Russia—it is a simple truism that two effective weapons in an arsenal are better than one. Having more optional stages in an escalation translates into control of an escalation towards the nuclear threshold and thus allows more strategic flexibility crucial for avoiding a nuclear exchange altogether—not to mention the fact that hypersonic weapons are effective conventional strategic deterrents and disruptors. The classic U.S. Navy's claim to Sea Control in the zones of deployment of such weapons becomes meaningless, since the only force capable of influencing the operational and strategic balance on the high seas will be U.S. Navy's superb world-class submarine force which, in absence of credible support from carrier air wings and surface combatants' air-defense capabilities, would be forced to face not only Russia's submarines but its Patrol/ASW aviation.

This is a situation which U.S. Navy hadn't faced in the 1970s and 1980s. In fact, the U.S. Navy never faced such a threat and such severe strategic ramifications as it concerns the U.S. geopolitical position. Even in the time of the Cold War it was still thought that the U.S. Navy would be able to overcome the Soviet Navy's "pincers," a.k.a. Flank Strategy, around Europe to provide the stream of manpower and war materiel across the Atlantic in case of war between NATO and the Warsaw Pact. Those times are gone because it's not in Russia's interest to "invade" Europe, though in case of war it will be able to provide a land "bridge" to the Kaliningrad Region which remains the only official exclave of the Russian Federation, and because the nature of war has changed. This fact, however, is precisely the one which Western elites are not yet capable to face and grapple with.

The fact that the Western political class is slow in grasping the new military reality, due to both hubris and the lack of a proper military backgrounds, was demonstrated in an almost comical way in March 2019 during NATO war-gaming which sought to address a possible escalation between Russia and Ukraine. The participants of these games, led by former NATO Secretary General Lord Robertson and including students of a Masters' Program in International Conflict and Cooperation, did not know the basic geography of the territory, and were basing their war-gaming on delusional premises, such as Ukraine joining NATO.

It was something to behold. That is, until one was presented with the "war planning," which among such pearls of strategic thinking included an utterly false assessment of Russia's capabilities and produced a dramatic manifestation of new NATO elites' utter military incompetence when it was concluded that:

> NATO action in Ukraine would be complicated by a low bridge that Russia has opened connecting Crimea to the Russian mainland. This makes it difficult for larger ships to move between Ukraine's Black Sea ports and the Mediterranean.[24]

At this stage one is forced to ask: what is the value of such "war-gaming" by students and political leaders, present and future, who do not have even a rudimentary understanding of the influence of complex modern combat technology on tactics, operations and strategy? People with Masters degrees or PhDs in economics, international relations and law, among other humanities fields, do not have the training to make good military analysts nor, especially, great military leaders—they simply have no tools for understanding modern warfare. The sheer absurdity of such a conclusion that the Crimean Bridge is an impediment to, presumably, NATO's "larger ships" passing into the Sea of Azov, of course, misses one very serious issue—in case of any real conventional war between NATO and Russia how many NATO "larger ships" are going to survive a perilous and militarily absolutely useless journey *towards* the Crimean Bridge? Never mind that Russians have resisted invading Ukraine since 2014, despite many calls to do so from inside Russia from people with as low geopolitical and military intelligence as those participating in such a mockery of war-gaming as that led by Lord Robertson.

In general, Western elites have huge issues of grasping the realities of a missile age. And, as the above example shows, it seems they will fail to do so in the future, still viewing the possibility of a conventional conflagration between NATO and Russia as very distant from any damage to London, Brussels or Washington D.C. Nothing could be further from the truth but that is what continues to constitute a main obstacle for many NATO and Pentagon planners—the myth of a completely secure rear in a conventional scenario.

Geographic Insularity: The Myth of the Secure Rear

Geographic insularity, that is to say, large distances from the enemy is no longer a decisive factor in a conventional, non-nuclear scenario. The mythology of the remoteness of conventional war theaters and thus safety of the rear was perpetuated by United States which proclaimed itself the "finest fighting force in history" based purely on the campaign against third rate Iraqi Army and military-strategic ineptness of Saddam Hussein himself.[25] The fact that U.S. military in its modern history never experienced any serious fire impact on its command and control centers and rear somehow was never discussed. That is, not until President Putin's speech to the Russian Federal Assembly on March 1, 2018—despite the fact that even before Russia's launching of the hypersonic missile age in warfare, even before its disclosures about the existence and deployment of such weapon systems as the *Kinzhal,* Russia possessed a conventional ability to devastate any military target in Europe, Middle East or U.S. proper. Russia had been deploying carriers of long-range cruise missiles at all strategic directions since 2014, as confirmed by Chief of General Staff Valery Gerasimov in 2018.[26] The whole notion of finding oneself, similarly to Saddam's army, with one's Command and Control completely disrupted, with one's sensors blinded and rear ammunition depots and pre-deployed forces under attack, is not something that many in the current U.S. political and even some military elites can easily imagine.

Moreover, Western elites, and American elites especially, are generally simply not in the frame of mind to view their countries and indeed themselves personally as possible and legitimate targets in case of a conventional war. Russians know, as an example, that President Putin even today could be a target for a variety of governmental and non-government groups—even in peace time. In case of war the Russian President, Prime Minister and the whole chain of command and national authority, including but not limited to MPs of both houses of Russian Parliament are aware that they would become targets automatically. Hence the significance of the whole notion that the accuracy of modern stand-off weapons is such that they can literally fly into the garage door of a house, making warfare also very personal, is a psychological barrier not many in the West have the ability to surmount—even though that is not just a capability of the future but a current reality of today's warfare, which is likely to become even more deadly and pointed.

Being located in a strategic depth far away from the line of contact of opposing forces guarantees very little in terms of personal safety anymore. But the American political class does not yet think in such terms—they simply have no reference points to regard themselves personally in danger, other than those American legislators who are former operational military personnel who have at least some grasp of the consequences of war itself, let alone even a conventional war between Russia and the United States. An overwhelming majority of the American legislators and political class are people from law, political science, journalism and business backgrounds with non-existent experiences in modern weapons, operational art and strategy. They simply cannot conceive of the fact that even in a conventional war scenario many Washington D.C. buildings could be attacked and destroyed. This is simply beyond any American experience, unless one wants to recall—as few do—the burning of Washington in 1814. Nowadays and into the nearest future events may unfold with such a lightning speed that there may not be enough time to even evacuate many people of critical importance. The mathematics demonstrating the possibility of successful evacuation, unless the evacuation is done in advance thus raising the degree of suspicion and tension, is simply not there, especially in the case of a salvo of hypersonic *Zircons* from vast off-coast areas—the time to escape will be measured in minutes for some, in seconds for others.

But for any conventional or nuclear scenario, deployment of cruise missiles with unlimited range, which have the ability to loiter for days, is yet another game changer. On February 16, 2019 Russia announced the successful completion of the state trials of a nuclear-powered engine for the *9M730 Burevestnik* (*Petrel*) cruise missile.[27] The 9M370 is a subsonic cruise missile whose nuclear propulsion gives it the ability to remain in the air for a very long time thus able to cover huge intercontinental distances while being able to attack from the most unexpected (for air defense) directions. Western, especially American, media were fast to dismiss the *Petrel* as undeployable based on, yet again, unnamed "intelligence sources" and dubious "intelligence reports" whose disastrous record of forecasts leaves very little doubt as to the simple sour-grapes/self-medicating nature of such "intelligence."[28] The U.S. media on the whole have an atrocious record when dealing with Russia in general and the Russian military in particular, continuously attempting to either downplay or dismiss Russia's capabilities, both military and economic, only to be later faced with the fact of its own fallacy. This is a Modus Operandi of most American media, part of which derives from cognitive dissonance in American journalists and pundits accustomed to presenting the United States as an exceptional, superlative nation but also inter alia from the generally extremely low educational level of the American journalist corps and talking heads which prevents balanced and competent assessments making their way into the American mainstream media. As a result, the American media is increasingly justifiably dismissed as crude propaganda, not least perpetrated by Pentagon.[29]

There is very little doubt that the propaganda campaign against the latest Russian weapons is a misinformation operation, granted a grossly unsuccessful one, once one considers that Vladimir Putin's March 1, 2018 speech was also initially met with dismissal among many quarters, only to be shortly thereafter taken extremely seriously, a reality which, apart from the appropriate due manifested in the mass-media later, was confirmed by the number of declarations of the intention of the U.S. to develop its own American hypersonic weapons. So, after all, the message was heard. Russia does not necessarily try hard to hide the tests of her new weapons and probably is unperturbed by U.S. reconnaissance and intelligence space-based assets accessing some telemetry on her newest missiles to dispel all doubts about their capabilities.

Unlike already deployed *Kinzhal, Avangard* or nearing deployment *Zircon,* the *Petrel* is unique, due to its unlimited range, as a vengeance weapon in case some among American decision-makers who may help precipitate a new world war might try to hide from the effects of what they have unleashed in the relative safety of Southern Hemisphere—the range will not be an obstacle for Petrel once reliable intelligence will be *provided.* This is a completely new paradigm for warmongers and hawks in Washington, most of whom, from draft dodgers Dick Cheney and John Bolton to ideologues of American exceptionalism and interventionism such as Robert Kagan, among many, saw weapons and war only on TV screens. That didn't prevent them from being the main ideologues behind inflicting horrendous losses and suffering on people around the globe.

While not yet enabling the future wars of assassins, as was envisioned for a more distant future by Frank Herbert in his Dune epic, this new military technology *makes* new warfare increasingly personal: the time when decision-makers could enjoy war making well-protected and far removed from the operations theater dugouts of a conventional conflict is coming to an end. Decision-centers and, with them, decision-makers, will be attacked and annihilated if they decide to do the unthinkable by unleashing a global conflict. Even in a conventional conflict, weapons will be coming from the most unexpected directions and they will be simply uninterceptable or detected too late for an effective defense.

The New Physics

Can weapons based on new physical principles be developed to counter this new hypersonic capability? Theoretically yes, and attempts are being made by all major participants of the arms race to develop such weapons. It seems obvious that particles or directed energy weapons could be such an answer. To start with, direct energy weapons can, if not shoot down, at least disable the sensors of hypersonic weapons thus reducing the probability of a hit. But as of now, every side in this race is far away from producing actual combat lasers capable of shooting down anything other than slow plastic-made propeller-driven drones from a very short range. In laser weapons a huge issue is attenuation due to weather conditions, which can degrade the laser's ability to stop the missile dramatically.

And then, of course, comes the issue of targeting itself. Targeting, that is training, laser weapons at targets flying with tremendous speeds requires an exceptional accuracy in developing allowances for weather conditions and providing extremely accurate azimuth (bearing) and elevation when dealing with missiles. This doesn't even take into account the possibility of countermeasures which could be applied against the sensitive targeting optics of such lasers. It is a known problem for everybody. The U.S. Navy is toying with the HELIOS program, which tries to integrate combat lasers with the AEGIS radar and tries to replace Close In Weapon Systems (CIWS) such as the venerable *Phalanx* with lasers. As was reported, however, there are serious issues:

> While HELIOS will integrate with the Aegis combat system, the admiral said, it still relies on its own dedicated power supply. In the long run, the Navy wants lasers that draw on the ship's regular electrical system, but modern ships have less and less power to spare as the Navy upgrades their electronics, particularly with the new Air & Missile Defense Radar (AMDR) going on the newest Arleigh Burke destroyers, the Flight III variant. It'll actually be easier to power a laser on the smaller frigates the Navy is about to buy, said Boxall, because that'll be a new class whose margin for growth hasn't yet been eaten up by upgrades. Ultimately, Navy leaders say they want a new cruiser design built for much high power levels.[30]

In other words, we all are still far away from the time when combat lasers will be able to reliably shoot down hypersonic or even high supersonic missiles, especially when one considers the variety of counter-measures which could be used to mitigate the laser's impact on the missile such as, inter alia, frame rotation and the use of high reflective materials, which will keep combat lasers as a niche weapon system for a long while. In the end, the M=9 hypersonic missile, once one considers the radio-horizon of such ships as destroyers of the *Arleigh Burke-class* of around 40 kilometers, can cover such a distance in less than 15 seconds, while other systems such as the *Kinzhal* or the M=4.2 capable *Kh-32* attack targets almost vertically, making any defense almost impossible with or without lasers—even if one considers augmentation of the battlefield by means of Cooperative Engagement Capability (CEC). In the end, the missile has to be physically damaged to such a degree that it stops being a threat—a problem which is not yet solved today and may not be solved for a fairly long time—by which time, new means and methods of delivery of deadly payloads will have been developed, thus continuously changing the tactical, operational, and strategic global landscape.

It took indeed a real revolution, going reliably over the hypersonic threshold and into ranges counted in thousands of kilometers to change not only military dynamics but the global balance of power, completely overturning all established models and assumptions about national power and the global status of nations—all of which has far reaching consequences for a world in which the United States can no longer dictate its will without fear of being itself vulnerable. Such times are gone forever and no amount of propaganda, self-medication and self-aggrandizing can continue to hide this fact from an increasing number of people globally. This is the way real revolutions happen. For history, the twelve years from 2007 to 2019 is an instant; it is not even that long of a time for a human life.

CHAPTER 6

Shield Trumps Sword: Today's Air-Space Battles

While estimates vary wildly, approximately 1,737 U.S. aircraft (not counting helicopters) have been lost to hostile actions between 1961 and 1973 in South East Asia, largely over Vietnam.[1] The majority of these losses were due to AAA (Anti-Air Artillery) and SAMs (Surface to Air Missiles). During almost 24 months of the *Rolling Thunder* operation the U.S. lost 881 aircraft; in 1967 alone, the United States lost 62 aircraft to SAMs while losing 205 to AAA.[2] In 1973, during the 19-days long Yom Kippur War, the Israeli Air Force lost over 100 aircraft, most of them to SAMs.[3] This is just a highly abbreviated list of Surface-to-Air missiles engaging all kinds of aerial threats from high value attack and fighter jet aircraft, to bombers, to cruise missiles since the early 1960s. The feature which unifies all entries in this list is the fact that all these surface-to-air missiles and the targeting and launch systems for them were and are Soviet/Russian made. Putting it in simpler, more straightforward language—Soviet/Russian Air Defense systems, when used by skilled operators, have an unrivaled combat history. No other nation has a comparable record of the use of such systems in combat and thus of gaining such a combat experience.

But there is also a subtle detail in all this combat experience—in Statistics and Theory of Probability it is called a *sample space*. Speaking in mathematical language a sample space is a collection of all possible outcomes. In the case of throwing two six-sided dice, the sample space contains

36 outcomes. In case of air defense (AD) systems it is not a trivial matter of a few outcomes with the AD system shooting down the target or missing it—there are a myriad of possibilities which constitute a huge variety of engagement scenarios and AD systems operations in combat, not excluding the possibility of the AD system's defeat and annihilation by the enemy. The number is intimidating, once one considers what is involved in modern anti-air combat and how complex modern AD systems are. A good analogy with the sampling is U.S. Navy's undeniable leadership, and by a huge margin, in the designing, operating and combat use of aircraft carriers. The U.S. Navy is good in that because it "consumed," that is encountered and reacted to, a large share of the possible outcomes over many decades of operating its aircraft carriers and their air wings. Experience in any field is a distillation of having dealt with as many possibilities in a sample space as possible. There are no rivals to the U.S. Navy's experience of carrier operations. The same is true for Soviet/Russian air-defense operations.

What is even more important is that unlike aircraft carriers, whose operational utility shrinks constantly due to the development of new weapon systems, such as Russia and China's latest anti-shipping missiles which are capable with high probability of destroying a carrier battle group, air-defense systems only grow in importance and utility. They also grow tremendously in their capabilities. They do so because, unlike modern aircraft carriers, missile technology is very far from exhausting its developmental potential, a reality underscored by the latest developments in the air-defense field. The popular cliché that in the eternal battle between a sword and a shield, the sword eventually will win, may no longer be true. This has everything to do with technological revolution and with the mathematics involved in operations.

The foundation of American military thought since the end of WW II until very recently rests on power projection. In layman's lingo power projection is the strategy (and the doctrine) of being able to invade anyone, anywhere, anytime, at U.S. government volition. It is not surprising that the U.S. House Armed Services Committee has a separate subcommittee on Sea Power and Projection Forces. The United States simply doesn't know any other type of warfare other than the expeditionary one in which U.S. forces attack places, be that Yugoslavia, Iraq or Libya, far removed from the U.S. proper. Today the kind of warfare the United States is most preoccupied with is what was originally (in 2010) known as *Air Sea Battle*, and later was renamed the *Joint Concept for Access and Maneuver in the Global Commons (JAM-CG)*.[4] While many in U.S. military establishment enthusiastically embraced this doctrine which allegedly addresses some issues of the skills required to fight peers or near peers, indicating China as its main target, some pundits accused this doctrine of being provocatively incentivizing to China's growing military capability.[5]

Militarily, however, *JAM-CG* is hardly a new concept in fighting doctrines even for the United States and is nothing more than a doctrine of trying to fight nations which can actually shoot back and defend themselves. At the core of it is an idea of "networked, integrated forces capable of attack-in-depth, destroy and defeat adversary forces (NIA/D3)."[6] As recent events demonstrated, China, who has her own hypersonic weapons program, will have little difficulty defending her own littoral and coast even against the mighty U.S. Navy, and takes her air-defense very seriously as part of her own A2/AD (Anti-Access/Area Denial) capability. *JAM-CG* is specifically looking for ways to overcome those, now proverbial, A2/AD "bubbles," but it has only one way of doing it—a massive barrage of TLAMs and other missiles at the enemy's military installations, especially its command and control centers and air-defense forces. To do so, the United States has at its disposal thousands of Tomahawk Land Attack Missiles (TLAM) of different versions which, together with combat aviation are at the core of American concept of warfare, which can be reduced to a simple, easily grasped stratagem of bombing the enemy into oblivion before any other forces, such as infantry, even appear near the area of operations. This is a very effective strategy for dealing with countries which have no means of defending themselves. Once, however, the nation which dared to anger the United States acquires a modern and integrated, in the full meaning of this word, air defense, not to speak of a capable air force, matters change dramatically for even the most advanced war-fighting doctrines—the air-defense shield becomes a formidable obstacle for the aggressive sword.

While on April 14, 2018, the U.S. media, known for its lack of integrity and inability to provide full and accurate facts, touted the U.S. and NATO allies' launching of a salvo of more than 100 TLAMs against Syria based on false reporting, the reality on the ground was far from triumphant. Syrian air defense forces managed to shoot down 71 out of the 103 land attack missiles.[7] The result was scandalous and in the West it created a huge controversy, which was expected, and a string of crude denials, also expected. As one senior American intelligence professional noted then, commenting on then Defense Secretary Mattis' unconvincing attempts to forestall and mitigate the effect of actual data being presented to public:

> The Russians and Syrians were not lying when they claimed to have downed more than 70 of the U.S., UK and French missiles. I understand the reluctance of the U.S. military leaders to admit the truth about

this debacle. It would undermine the confidence of the American people is our supposedly invincible weapon systems and would embarrass and enrage the man child that inhabits the White House. Better to tell him lies and let him believe the fantasy. But this is a very dangerous game. So far the Russians have not pursued significant PR efforts to expose the U.S. lie about the missiles. Maybe they are choosing to keep quiet, like a good poker player, and not tip their hand to the American public. One of these days Trump and company will over bet in trusting the Russians not to punch back (and punch back hard) and the American people will be in for a rude awakening. They will discover that the Russians have a decided advantage over us when it comes to air defense."[8]

Eventually, the data even trickled down into Western media. The result in Syria was historic in a sense that it was achieved by upgraded but still old Soviet air-defense systems. Neither the S-400 nor the S-300 systems deployed by Russia in Syria were engaged in combat mode on this occasion. NATO's failure was embarrassing but it was also very instructive, since it clearly pointed to the very low combat effectiveness of the main American strike weapons, TLAMs, when used against even a more-or-less well trained opponent which has at least some means to defend itself and is provided good targeting—in case of April 13, 2018 strikes most likely by Russian electronic means deployed in Syria—such as Syria's modern Russian-made *S1 Pantsir* air-defense complexes, perfectly fit for defending against low-flying targets such as *Tomahawks*. What would have been the performance of TLAMs against an opponent such as China which not only has its own domestically-produced versions of the Russian S-300 air-defense complexes but is buying the S-400, is difficult to forecast. Most likely the U.S. will not have enough Tomahawks to break through serious modern, multi-layered air-defenses which makes operational considerations of *JAM-CG* mostly a pipe dream.

China is aware of her geographic vulnerability, with a majority of her population and her industries concentrated in a relatively narrow strip along her coast, thus requiring a powerful integrated air-defense. So China bought $3 billion-worth of *S-400 Triumphs* from Russia and immediately tested them using a ballistic target with a speed of 3 kilometers per second. The target was successfully shot down at the distance of 250 kilometers.[9] The maximum range of the S-400 is around 400 kilometers, which is achieved when a 40N6E missile is used. The S-400 is ideally suited to deal with exact type of strike assets the United States would use in case of a conventional conflict with China, which continues to build its own multi-layered air defense capable to defend against anything the United States may launch against Chinese targets. The S-400, as well as the older but very capable *S-300PMU2 Favorit* systems, are fully capable of detecting, tracking and engaging so-called VLO (Very Low Observability) or Stealth targets. Such capability is achieved by sensor fusion and modern signal processing techniques. China today has access to this technology which, together with Chinese copies of Russian systems or indigenous Chinese systems, creates a serious impediment for any attack on China's shores.

A primary proof of the immense success of Russian air-defense systems is the line of customers wanting to buy export versions of the S-400. India has already signed a $5 billion dollar contract for the S-400, despite political pressure against so doing from the U.S.[10] But if India was not a pushover, the saga between the United States and Turkey, who signed the contract for deliveries of the S-400 from

Russia gives a new meaning to the definitions of both sour grapes and the lack of U.S. competitiveness in the field of air-defense. The fact that Turkey, a key NATO member, signed the contract, and Qatar, a home for forward headquarters of the U.S. CENTCOM and the largest air force base in the region, is in discussion with Russia for buying the S-400, became a constant and very serious irritant for Washington. The United States resorted to direct blackmail of Turkey in order to stop Ankara from taking a delivery of S-400s from Russia.[11] For starters, the United States halted deliveries of its F-35 fighter to Turkey in an attempt to prevent a NATO ally from buying Russian air-defense complexes. Its justification for halting F-35 deliveries was at best laughable—the halt was justified in these terms:

> The United States and other NATO allies that own F-35s fear the radar on the Russian S-400 missile system will learn how to spot and track the jet, making it less able to evade Russian weapons in the future.[12]

The sheer absurdity of this justification is manifested by its technical ignorance, since most modern Russian long-range air-defense complexes of the S-300 or S-400 family already have organic capabilities to detect, track and shoot down stealth targets. These are achieved by a complex of measures: different bands of radar, sensor fusion algorithms, and modern signal processing, among others. This may explain why the United States and the Israeli Air Force are very evasive when commenting on the potential use of F-35 and F-22 fighters in Syria and their possible encounter with Syrian air defense forces. As one observer noted, commenting on a rumor of Israeli Air Force F-35 being hit by a Syrian missile of the old S-200 air-defense complex:

The interesting part is that the F-35 has become such a symbol of U.S. technological prowess—or incompetence—that any rumor that an F-35 has been damaged or shot down in combat will draw attention.[13]

Here is the problem, a psychological one: with the constant extolling and exaggerating of combat capability of one's own technology, the expectations bar is raised so high, especially when reinforced by non-stop media and entertainment propaganda, that even a relatively insignificant combat hiccup has a tendency to grow into a major public issue. The notion that the U.S. Air Force can sustain appalling losses, including in her vaunted "stealth" aircraft, or that the U.S. Navy's Carrier Battle Group can simply be destroyed, when encountering near peer or peer in war, is so beyond the emotional grasp of the American political elite and most of the general public, that on some occasions even robust professionals have to make statements and draw conclusions which only raise eyebrows. In 2017 a group of RAND Corporation's researchers, headed by one of the RAND's authorities on combat aviation, David Ochmanek, in their study *U.S. Military Capabilities and Forces for a Dangerous World. Rethinking the U.S. Approach to Force Planning*, came to an astonishing conclusion. After lengthy blaming of Russia for complicating U.S. efforts in *"use of air power and SOF units to inflict damage on ISIS,"* and for other Russian mischiefs such as non-existent "hybrid warfare,"[14] they calculated the required force for defeating Russia in a scenario RAND called *One Major War*. After waxing geopolitical and extolling, as usual, U.S. Armed Forces as the finest fighting force in the world, Ochmanek and his group, by juggling all kinds of facts and techno-fantasies, decided that to "defeat" Russia the U.S. will need 28 fighter squadrons and 7 bomber squadrons, or in general, around 760-800 aircraft of all types.[15]

That raises an immediate question, or rather a host of questions, with answers for such a scenario as follows:

Q. When was the last time the USAF fought in a highly dense EW environment with AD systems whose capabilities covered ALL challenges which are presented by the latest in U.S. technology, itself?

A. Never. In fact, the USAF may not even have internalized it yet, that it *will* (not may) fight blind with its Command, Control and Communications (C3) either seriously challenged or completely disrupted.

Q. When was the last time the USAF fought a world-class adversary AF which can approach or match the USAF on the theater both in the quality of its pilots and aircraft, and in their quantity?

A. Never, since Korea.

Q. When was the last time the USAF deployed to the front-line, or even rear, airbases which were subjected to major attacks by both an adversary's AF and salvos of cruise and tactical operational high precision stand-off weapons, which led to a severe disruption of that adversary's air operations, massive casualties of personnel and significant loss of its aircraft?

A. Never. After observing a rather unimpressive performance (OK, failure) of the Patriot anti-missile systems against obsolete 1970s Yemeni Scud knock-offs recently, one is forced to ask: what will this AD do against a state-of-the-art, stealthy, AI-driven and EW-resistant missiles salvo, say of 40 or 60 missiles? How about several such salvos?

Q. Does Mr. Ochmanek understand that the myth of Stealth has been completely dispelled and that modern AD complexes and advanced radar systems of modern aircraft such as the *SU-30SM, SU-35C* or *MiG-31BM* can see, track and shoot down any "Stealth" target?

A. Maybe.

Q. Does this RAND group calculate U.S. attrition rates in such conflict correctly?

A. No. Anyone who thinks that a force of around 800 good but fairly conventional (or really bad) combat aircraft can go up against Russian Air-Space Forces in Russia's vicinity and win is either disingenuous or incompetent. The USAF will not be able to suppress Russia's AD system to start with; the opposite, degrading of USAF EW and kinetic capabilities, most likely will be true.

But the bigger issue here is that the mathematics is simply not there. It never was since the late 1960s, and especially is not today, when Russia's VKS (Air-Space Forces) deploys an astonishing array of weapons both kinetic and electronic, including laser weapons, capable of dramatically degrading even an alpha-strike of all NATO's forces in Europe on Russia. In the end, the air war is still an integral part of a "major war" which in case of Russia, and China, would be conducted in four domains: ground, air, space and sea. The dynamics of such a war will depend primarily on the actions of fully integrated ground, air-space and naval forces, all of which, in the case of Russia, are capable of defeating conventionally any combination of threats in Russia's vicinity. The self-medicating and largely propaganda nature of RAND's study became obvious when this very same David Ochmanek was forced to admit in 2019, a year and a half later, that RAND's war games which pitted the United States and her allies against Russia and China ended in catastrophe for the "finest fighting force in the world" under most scenarios. In fact, he admitted:

> We lose a lot of people. We lose a lot of equipment. We usually fail to achieve our objective of preventing aggression by the adversary. In our games, when we fight Russia and China, blue gets its ass handed to it.[16]

RAND Corporation, known for its incessant push for more money for the Pentagon, still, at least openly, doesn't get a simple fact of real warfare with serious adversaries—the rate of attrition. The issue is not just the quantity of personnel and equipment being lost but the speed, the rate, with which those losses will accumulate. A constant referencing the United States' Armed Forces having conventional superiority over Iraqi, Taliban or Libyan forces, other than a nauseating repetition of the obvious, does nothing to convey the scale of actual losses for NATO air forces in the case of encountering Russian air-defenses and air-force, while at the same time dealing with what no NATO country in general, and the U.S. in particular, has ever experienced in recent history—a sustained attack on their air fields, EW centers, Command and Control infrastructure and forces in the field. This type of conflict has no precedent in U.S. military history and unfortunately, this is not the reality anyone in authority in the U.S. feels the necessity to disclose to the American public in general—the "finest fighting force," "stealth" and other exceptionalist American military mythology must be preserved at all costs, since the public's learning this reality may have far reaching consequences for the current American elites.

The emergence of Russia's latest air-defense systems, however, will spell doom for U.S. Air Force air operations as such and will require a complete rethinking of its force structure and of fighting doctrine. This may not be at all easy with the S-500 anti-missile complex entering full combat capability, which is networked with the already deployed S-400 and other systems. The S-500 is capable of deploying exo-atmospheric interceptors for ballistic missiles and for shooting down satellites at low orbits, but it is its range against aero-dynamic targets which re-defines the rules of modern air-combat: the S-500 is capable of reaching

AWACS planes. While CNBC's citing any kind of news on the Russian military by its own journalist, Amanda Macias, and her allegedly "informed U.S. intelligence sources"— ever-unnamed—is nothing more than rumor-mongering or outright disinformation, including her statement about the S-500 shooting down a target that she claimed was 299 miles away[17] (Russia's S-400 has already downed an air target in tests at the range of 400 kilometers), there is very little doubt in the case of the S-500 that the system was designed from the outset as a new world in terms of its range and the speed of its intercepted targets. Some sources claim that the S-500 is even capable of intercepting hypersonic non-ballistic targets.

The already immense and confirmed range of 400 kilometers at which Russia's S-400 downed an air target in tests is precisely the kind of range at which the radar of the AWACS aircraft operates. It is also the range (at around 320 kilometers) at which the large and very visible for radar at which AWACS planes such as the Boeing E-3 Sentry will have to operate in order to provide crucial reconnaissance, command and control, and EW capability for air operations of its own force.[18] This dramatically increases the probability of being able to deny the attacking force's command and control and reconnaissance through highly mobile and very long range air-defense complexes such as the S-400 or the S-500. This is what is so revolutionary in those systems. Exclusion zones for AWACS aircraft thus become zones where NATO's aircraft will have to fight in a highly dense Russian EW environment while being denied proper vectoring and targeting, even as the Russian air force will operate its own well-defended Beriev A-50U and A-100 Airborne Early Warning and Control planes.

The S-500, together with latest middle-range state-of-the-art air-defense system S-350 Vityaz are nearing their operational status, planned for 2020, and crews for them are already in training.[19] Combined with its growing anti-satellite capability, Russia's VKS (Air-Space Forces) even in standalone mode represents a formidable, possibly unsurmountable obstacle for any combination of forces and any contemporary fighting doctrine attempting to conduct air-space operation against Russia proper and her vicinity. Unfortunately, this doesn't mean that such attempts, as may be announced or promoted through the mainstream media, will not be made. This current situation is not exactly one the United States is used to, since it undermines its exceptionalist military narrative at its very foundation and this is abhorrent to a society obsessed with violence and militarism. Yet, as some American professionals are forced to grudgingly admit:

> The era of U.S. technological dominance is over. Indeed, in many areas, including military technology, the gap has narrowed to parity or near-parity.[20]

The reality is more complex than the United States simply facing overall "parity." There is no parity between Russia and the United States in such fields as air-defense, hypersonic weapons and, in general, missile development, to name just a few fields—the United States lags behind in these fields, not just in years but in generations. How, then, did this happen that the nation which is the birthplace of modern aviation and is rightly proud about it, got it so wrong about the direction of evolution of modern air, space and air-defense forces? At least a substantial part of the answer to this puzzle lays with the United States infatuation with the power of flight, yet the United States was hardly the only nation that, at the dawn of aviation, went through an obsessive attachment to aviation—the Soviet Union went through it, as did Germany, France and Great Britain, among few other nations. As U.S. Air Force Lt. Colonel Barry D. Watts warned in 1984:

> The fundamental thinking of U.S. aviators about the air weapon, be it airplane or nuclear missile, has long been beset by certain shortcomings. First and foremost, as professional soldiers we have failed to nurture a comprehensive understanding of war as a total phenomenon... These shortcomings raise legitimate doubts, I believe, as to the capacity of the U.S. Air Force to do the one thing that successful military organizations have always done: *adapt to changing conditions better than the adversary*. Unless we, as professional airmen, develop a more adequate understanding of war as a totality, and unless we manage to attain some measure of objectivity, of informed historical perspective regarding our more deeply held beliefs about the air weapon, I would question our ability to adapt successfully to the demands of American security in the late 20th century."[21]

The upshot flows from Watt's conclusion: the United States in general doesn't adapt better to changing conditions than the adversary and it has serious issues with historical perspective. Until recently, the United States was the only major nation which believed that the air force alone could win the war. In this sense, the United States was and still largely remains a dedicated follower of the moribund Gioulio Douhet and Billy Mitchel doctrines of air war, of which strategic bombing is the foundation. The absurdity of the thesis that air power alone can win a war was and is evident for people with even rudimentary knowledge of warfare of the 20th and 21st century and with what Lt. Colonel Watts calls an understanding of "war as a total phenomenon." This thesis of air power omnipotence received such a wide circulation, especially among lay public in the U.S., due to the U.S. and Coalition destroying Saddam's forces in the Gulf in 1991, bombing them into oblivion without any resistance, that in 1999 Slate magazine felt compelled to address this gross misunderstanding of warfare:

> Many pundits are criticizing the NATO airstrikes. An argument you often hear is that "Air strikes alone never work." Is this really true? Most military historians (at least those not employed by the U.S. Air Force) agree that it's true. No country has ever won a war or achieved its stated political objectives without committing ground troops or at least using warships. Moreover, some historians make the even stronger claim that air power has never been a *decisive* factor in a military conflict. To take one example, scholars think Japan surrendered in 1945 because of the Allied naval blockade and Russia's invasion of Manchuria, rather than because of atomic and conventional bombings.[22]

Yet the vision of hi-tech armadas of aircraft pummeling America's enemies into utter submission gripped the nation in the aftermath of the WW II, with the real mechanisms and scale of the effort behind the defeat of Axis powers falling victim to the ideological imperatives of unfolding Cold War and the American narrative of the U.S. entry being key to the victory. The fact that the Nazi military machine was primarily destroyed at the Eastern Front in the bloodiest warfare in history, with gigantic infantry, tank and air armies fighting as unified forces against each other, was removed not only from American public considerations but was dramatically downgraded even in the American professional military environment by means of what Atkinson defined, while speaking about General George Patton, as "the creeping arrogance, the hubris, which would cost the American Army so dearly in Vietnam."[23] Even Vietnam's experience with the emerging SAM threat to air operations didn't really shake American faith in the omnipotence of air power. And indeed, it was almost omnipotent against nations with no means to effectively defend themselves. The legends of U.S. Air Power being a decisive factor in WW II, at least at the Western Front, continued to be disseminated well into the 21st century, based on the *United States Strategic Bombing Survey (USSBS)* results published in Autumn of 1945. The conclusion of the survey was unequivocal:

> Allied air power was decisive in the war in Western Europe. Hindsight inevitably suggests that it might have been employed differently or better in some respects. Nevertheless, it was decisive. In the air, its victory was complete. At sea, its contribution, combined with naval power, brought an end to the enemy's greatest naval threat—the U-boat; on land, it helped turn the tide overwhelmingly in favor of Allied ground forces. Its power and superiority made possible the success of the invasion. It brought the economy which sustained the enemy's armed forces to virtual collapse, although the full effects of this collapse had not reached the enemy's front lines when they were overrun by Allied forces. It brought home to the German people the full impact of modern war with all its horror and suffering. Its imprint on the German nation will be lasting.[24]

The very suggestion that the success of the Allied landing in Normandy depended primarily on the efforts of the Red Army tying massive Axis armies at the Eastern Front, as was decided at the Tehran Conference in 1943 and in the inter-Allied strategic deliberations, is received by many in the U.S. with disbelief.[25] The pondering on the omnipotence of air power continues in the United States even today, thus providing for endless discussion on the ability of air power alone to win wars. Questions such as *Could Air Power Have Won the Vietnam War?* are being debated even today.[26] The answer, however, lies in the simple truth which was clearly stated by experienced U.S. Navy's aviators in 2001, that "foreign adversaries will have SAM systems that manned aircraft cannot approach (after some 'Pearl Harbor' event for manned aircraft)."[27] If one were to view Russia as America's adversary—a rather huge issue whose possible unexpected results should be pondered by those in the U.S. who do view Russia as enemy—the era of SAM systems which are unapproachable by American, or any other, manned aircraft has arrived and it did so a long time ago. Nor will the new air power fad of swarms of small UAVs, or drones, which may accompany and be controlled from such aircraft as F-35s change the power equation significantly—in an EW dense environment swarms of UAVs will have their communications partially suppressed or completely disrupted and will have their sensors disabled. While UAVs are here to stay and are an important part of the new technological paradigm, one should never lose the sight of a simple truism that SAMs, anti-shipping missiles or any other SMART munitions are, in essence, drones of different capabilities.

Air war has changed today and it changed in a revolutionary way, a way that what can broadly be defined as U.S. air power doctrine, didn't foresee—leading to attrition rates beyond anything the U.S. Air Force ever encountered in the post-WW II era. Space-based assets are no longer untouchable. The development of anti-satellite weapons proceeds apace, with lately India joining the club of nations with anti-satellite capability after shooting down a satellite at low-Earth orbit on March 27, 2019.[28] Under these circumstances, the only question the United States must ask itself when assessing the risks of involving itself in yet another failed military adventure is—how fast will the global proliferation of advanced SAM systems and air force capabilities proceed? This is not an idle question—modern SAM systems, advanced EW systems which can be integrated with them, and the required training of personnel is no longer beyond the grasp of middle-level geopolitical players.

The long saga related to the delivery of S-300 PMU1 SAM systems from Russia to Iran is a testimony to the extreme sensitivity of U.S. and Israeli air forces to even legacy Russian systems reaching the perimeter of the Eurasian Continent. Israel, and her U.S.-based influence groups, for years expressed a great deal of concern about the Russian-Iranian contract for S-300 delivery and exerted political pressure on Russia in order to sabotage those deliveries, delaying them until 2016.[29] Russian-made S-400s are also proliferating to the Eurasian perimeter, from China to India, to Syria, and possibly, to Turkey. Iran and Iraq also expressed the desire to purchase S-400 complexes. These systems, apart from their direct threat to U.S. air operations against nations which have such systems, have, however, a deeper meaning which is purely economic—they expose the U.S. huge investment into so-called Stealth technologies as a technological and operational mistake of massive proportions and threaten, in an era of the U.S. losing its grip on its allies and enemies alike, both its reputation and its commercial interest in promoting U.S. designed and manufactured combat aviation globally. Today the primary American product for sale is the F-35, whose combat and the so-called Stealth capabilities seem to be grossly overstated. Even many U.S. NATO allies are not enthusiastic about paying astronomical sums for a plane with a mediocre performance and dubious survivability in real conflict.[30]

The proliferation of SAM systems is just one facet of a general rearmament of the Eurasian geographic fringes and outliers. Russian combat aviation is a "hot" item on many markets—a result which was achieved through Russia's Syria campaign in which Russian combat aviation played a crucial role in helping to turn the tide of war in Syria in 2015 and then aided Syrian, Iranian and Russian ground forces in defeating the Islamic State. Even Egypt not only wants Russia's SAM systems but in a dramatic move signed a $2 billion contract with Russia for more than 20 *Sukhoi SU-35* fighter jets, whose performance in Syria was cited as one of the major reasons for Egypt deciding to go along with this advanced aircraft. As Andrew Korybko noted:

> Speaking of the Sinai and gas reserves, those are actually two of the main reasons why Egypt wants Russian fighter jets in the first place. The Su-35s proved their worth wiping out terrorists in Syria, which obviously makes them very attractive assets for aiding Egypt's anti-terrorist operations in the Sinai, but also in protecting its porous borders with Libya and Sudan from the worst-case scenario of Daesh or a similar entity trying to storm across and recreate a so-called "caliphate." Concerning energy security, it's more cost-effective for Egypt to protect its offshore gas reserves with airpower that could also be wielded in other domains such as the anti-terrorist one than to invest unnecessary funds in modernizing its fleet. All told, the $2 billion Su-35 deal will therefore go a long

way towards enhancing Egypt's strategic security in parallel with expanding Russia's influence in North Africa.[31]

Needless to say, Washington was not happy with Egypt buying state-of-the-art Russian planes and applied political pressure—by now a familiar pattern, indeed, Washington's modus operandi when dealing with the proliferation of Russian-made hi-end weapon systems.[32] The explanation of the American growing irritation and, as a consequence, irrational self-defeating application of political pressure on any customer seeking Russia's advanced military technology is rather simple—the dawning realization of the United States that it is losing the conventional arms race to Russia, and, possibly to China, due to its arrogance, myopia and inability to learn and apply lessons based on hard facts and calculations, rather than its self-created mythology. This is especially true in the field where the United States self-proclaimed to be the most advanced and powerful force in the world: aerospace. All that was done by dismissing the economic, technological and geopolitical reality which formed in front of the very eyes of the American political class, which simply lacked the required orientation and tools to properly assess an unfolding real revolution in military affairs that the United States was neither ready nor willing to acknowledge—the increasing gap between indigenous, grossly propaganda-inflated exceptionalist military capabilities and the military-technological revolution the U.S. "peers" were undergoing. Russia, in the words of Lt. Colonel Watts, indeed *adapted to changing conditions better than the adversary.*

Chapter 7

The Global Impact of the
Proliferation of New Military Technologies

After even brief considerations of most of the factors shaping military-political reality today one cannot fail to start asking questions about the current state of American geopolitical modelling and its most significant lacunae.

Indeed, where is the crucial index for air and space defense forces in the model inspired by RAND and used by Russian applied mathematicians who follow RAND in this index of military power:

$$X_M = 0.5 X_{M1}[0.5(X_{M2} + X_{M3}) + X_{M4}]$$

Apart from the deliberately misleading, if not meaningless, M1 index (a nation's share in global military expenditures), this model not only ignores strategically and operationally critical air-space defense but while doing so, forgets yet another crucial index, that of air forces, which cannot be merely "included" into the generic M2 index (the military potential of a nation's army). How realistically do such factors as state-of-the-art air defense or massive EW capabilities influence this potential? No "model" concocted in economic or allegedly geopolitical Western think-tanks provides for a real—and public—assessment of those factors. As was stated previously, any capability to distort or altogether disable U.S. GPS entails a dramatic loss of combat effectiveness of U.S. military power. Russia has such a capability, which, yet again, following Admiral Turner's dictum, is a capability to do what's needed in particular situation. While still expensive such capabilities are on an order of magnitude cheaper than the entire mechanism of targeting employed by the U.S. Not to mention the fact that Russian Air Force has the ability to detect, track and intercept stand-off weapons.

So, in this case, of an un-nuanced index of "military potential of the army," not to speak of largely meaningless military expenses? It is especially surprising that such factors related to air power were ignored in the U.S., a nation which is obsessed with it.

In the end, all quantitative and, on the surface, so-called qualitative factors forming contemporary military reality and, by extension, geopolitical status rest on these simple principles:

- The military potential of a nation is first a derivative of the complexity and size of its economy. Such an economy must be very advanced in order to be able to have world-class armed forces.
- Military potential does not translate into military victories directly.
- It is how military potential is deployed, becomes kinetic, that is, which in the end defines the real and geopolitical power of the nation.

We have primarily addressed this issue by comparing the United States and Russia, but the findings of the paradigm don't change when applied to other conflict situations. Should this have been otherwise, the genocidal war by Saudi Arabia, whose armed forces on paper have massive potential against Yemen, would have come to a victorious conclusion years ago. This, however, is not the case. Having the most expensive armed forces in the Middle East, with the military budget of Saudi Arabia equaling that of Russia, one would expect this factor be decisive, but it is not.[1] Even a brief overview of Saudi-led military operations in Yemen provides evidence of its deliberate targeting of civilian infrastructure and concerted efforts to spread chaos and misery—hardly a sign of a truly advanced military. As *The New York Times* reported:

> In 2016, the Saudi-backed Yemeni government transferred the operations of the central bank from the Houthi-controlled capital, Sana, to the southern city of Aden. The bank, whose policies are dictated by Saudi Arabia, a senior Western official said, started printing vast amounts of new money—at least 600 billion riyals, according to one bank official. The new money caused an inflationary spiral that eroded the value of any savings people had. The bank also stopped paying salaries to civil servants in Houthi-controlled areas, where 80 percent of Yemenis live. With the government as the largest employer, hundreds of thousands of families in the north suddenly had no income."[2]

This is a tactic typical of warfare at its ugliest—now sexed up by the term "hybrid war" invented by Mark Galeotti and purporting to reflect the latest in contemporary understanding of the multiplicity of factors deployed in warfare. This method of financial destruction was practiced, one example among many, by Napoleon against Russia prior to his invasion in 1812 by attempting to flood Russia with counterfeit money.[3] With the Saudi intervention in Yemen now in its fifth year, one is forced to ask what have Saudi forces actually achieved by bombing civilian facilities and imposing a blockade largely responsible for a horrendous humanitarian catastrophe in Yemen? The answer seems to be self-evident—very little, given the collection of advanced military technology, mostly American and West European, at Saudi Arabia's disposal. As Colonel Patrick Lang noted prophetically at the start of Saudi-led intervention in Yemen in 2015:

> Saudi Arabia lacks the military capability to intervene successfully in Yemen. This is equally true in what was North Yemen (YAR) and also in the former PDRY. SA's armed forces were always built for show with a lot of expensive equipment that they were never capable of employing except at the elementary "stick and rudder" level of operations.[4]

Saudi intervention in Yemen is a classic case of having a very impressive X_M (index of military power) for a country of its size, while having no ability to deploy its potential properly and effectively. After all, in some military power rankings Saudi Arabia ranks as number 25, above Sweden and Belarus, and very close to Vietnam.[5] Yet, Saudi's $70 billion-dollar military budget is practically useless, even against the grossly outgunned Shia militias of Yemen. It is not surprising then, that even such a significant military potential— represented by many advanced shiny military toys, and a PPP GDP of $1.8 trillion dollars, albeit only marginally larger than that of Iran—does not make Saudi Arabia feel secure vis-à-vis her main geopolitical rival.[6] It is also obvious that Saudi GDP is primarily based on oil exports and the extraction and processing industries related to this export. Other than oil and its byproducts—and even that largely dependent on Western technologies and expertise— Saudi Arabia imports everything else, weapons included. In case of real war with serious adversary such as Iran, without Western support, Saudi Arabia's Armed Forces would degrade fast, without a chance of being replenished with new equipment and war materiel.

Primarily Western economic and military estimation analytical tools do not work anymore; they do not work because they stopped being grounded in reality. As one of the leading and highly influential contemporary Russian thinkers Sergei Mikheev bluntly put it on live radio—modern American economic science is rubbish, as is the gospel of free and fair trade.[7] It is very difficult to disagree with Mikheev here. Even in the hypothetical scenario of war between Saudi Arabia and Iran, one has to consider the actual face value of power for both. While the GDP structure of both countries is very similar, with oil exports dominating in both, the gap in actual military or fire power between the two is very large.[8] Iran ranks at the 14th place near relatively capable Egypt (12th place) and above Spain, Canada and Australia.[9]

While one may argue regarding Iran's ranking, very few informed people would argue with the fact that Iran is able to maintain and supply, through a network of native defense contractors, a relatively capable military force with a regional reach. And here one has only to conduct a mental forensic experiment asking which of these powers, Iran or Saudi Arabia, would be an easier target in case of full out conventional war for the United States, if she were to decide that she needs to "democratize" either Iran or Saudi Arabia. It is in instances such as this where the Global Status model, being discussed in this book, breaks down completely. It is not a far-fetched assumption that, in case of the U.S. deciding to fight Saudi Arabia, such a war would be very close to repetition of the First Gulf War due to the gigantic power mismatch between Saudi and U.S. armed forces. In other words, the U.S. will easily be able to defeat and occupy Saudi Arabia. (Mind you, what happens after that is a completely different story.) The case of Iran, however, is much more complex. Iran has more military resources than Saudi Arabia, it has larger population and, most importantly,

Iran is ready to fight. Bear in mind that this is a nation whose economy is nominally smaller than that of Saudi Arabia and has been under different strict sanctions regimes since 1979.

No less an authority than former Chief of Staff of Colin Powell, Colonel Lawrence Wilkerson, summarized a possible war with Iran as entailing a futile bombing campaign with the U.S. losing the war against Iran from the get go, especially if it decides to invade.[10] The explanation to this rather grim, and correct, prediction is very simple: Iran will be fighting as a unified nation at home. Of course, Iran's very complex terrain—a factor which is absent from the models discussed herein, which merely address area—would make any full-scale invasion by the U.S. an immediate throwback to the Vietnam War era and possibly see levels of ground troops attrition even higher. What then will be the worth of all models and assessments if, allegedly, the superpower and "finest fighting force in history" will have to face Iran on her territory? Not to be outdone, in 2013 Federation of American Scientists (FAS) came up with cost estimates for full blown invasion of Iran—the results, $2.8 trillion of costs for global economy in first three months of invasion.[11]

Such estimates have been done with full conviction that the process will proceed as follows:

> The United States resolves to invade, occupy, and disarm Iran. It carries out all of the above missions and goes "all in" to impose a more permanent solution by disarming the regime. Although the purpose of the mission is not explicitly regime change, the United States determines that the threat posed by Iran to Israel, neighboring states, and to freedom of shipping in the Strait of Hormuz cannot be tolerated any longer. It imposes a naval blockade and a no-fly zone as it systematically takes down Iran's military bases and

destroys its installations one by one. Large numbers of ground troops will be committed to the mission to get the job done.[12]

It is surprising how, yet again, this potential for war was viewed in the U.S. as merely applicable to its financial costs "spreadsheet," without considering:

1. The extent of U.S. losses in war materiel and lives;
2. The geopolitical consequences of such an endeavor.

Yet, this predictive lacuna is the inevitable result of the majority of Western elites' failure to grasp all the dimensions that real combined arms warfare conflict against even a weaker power such as Iran would entail. This simplistic scenario was outlined in 2013. Today in 2019 all operational and strategic assumptions about possible U.S. invasion of Iran are no longer valid. While some U.S. outlets did warn about possibly prohibitive costs of invading Iran, they missed one very serious factor:[13] an unfolding and very real Revolution in Military Affairs. With Iran in particular it wasn't just a matter of the delivery of the long promised S-300, whose upgraded versions, together with earlier deliveries of Tor-M2 systems, are being delivered starting from 2016, but the fact that Iran's ability to close off the Strait of Hormuz stopped being just a bluster. Iran has decisively entered the missile age and in the past decade, both out of its own resources and through technology transfer from China, has deployed an impressive array of mobile anti-shipping missile complexes capable to close off the entire Persian Gulf. This would create not only a huge operational challenge to the U.S. Navy's carrier battle groups in case of war but also would drive up the price of oil, and with it global political instability, to unacceptable levels. One can only imagine what the appearance of Russia's more recent *P-800 Onyx* (*Yakhont*) missiles can do to the operational regime in Persian Gulf and Gulf of Oman.

This fact brings a warranted and, in fact, irresistible question to the fore—what are the real ramifications of the proliferation of latest missile and other modern military technologies? The answer to this is as simple as it is complex and could be distilled to this simple truism—the current self-proclaimed hegemon does not have the means to intercept hypersonic weapons. These weapons are now highly desired by many countries—Turkey, Pakistan, India, China, even Hezbollah[14]—who understand their meaning and influence on modern warfare and, by implication, on their own security. Take India. Not only is India producing her own version of the deadly *P-800 Onyx* missile, named *BrahMos,* after the Russia-India Joint Venture, in its turn named after the Moskva (Moscow) and Brahmaputra rivers, but India is on her way of joining the exclusive club of nations with hypersonic missile capabilities.[15] Such capabilities change the geopolitical calculus dramatically and not in the favor of the United States and her allies who have largely followed the American approach to war for decades, both doctrinally and as customers—often coerced ones—of U.S. military technology.

It is difficult to fully explain the Pentagon's insensitivity to the outside stimuli, which seems to be almost deliberately induced, and its propensity for looking askance on real and potential adversaries' capabilities, but some voices bemoaning the U.S. lag in modern warfare were heard even before Russia unveiled her arsenal of hypersonic weapons. As one outlet, lamenting the U.S. lag behind China in 2014, commented while reviewing a new Chinese anti-shipping missile:

The arrival of the YJ-12 is one more indication of how the U.S. Navy is falling further behind in the missile competition against China, exposing flaws in operating concepts that U.S. and allied commanders and policymakers have relied on for years.[16]

By mid-2020 the U.S. lag in anti-shipping weapons will, most likely, become even greater. While warfare enablers, such as C4I (Command, Control, Computers, Communications and Intelligence) remain relatively strong points of the U.S. military arsenal, they are no longer untouchable, and in fact are being challenged constantly. But enablers are called such precisely since they are merely enablers of weapons, not the weapons themselves—and here the picture for the United States looks grim. In case of a serious war U.S. combat enablers will be degraded or suppressed, and as a result, the U.S. and its allies will be left outranged, outpaced and outgunned in a scenario which cannot reach the general public because of its massive political implications. Some American military pundits are still extolling the values of American combat networks and weapons operating at the machine, i.e., computer, speeds. This is an illusion. Chinese, and especially Russian, combat networks can also operate at machine (computer) speeds, while deploying weapons which are vastly superior to what U.S. combat networks operate today or will be able to in the foreseeable future. Enablers are only as good as the weapons they enable. The proliferation of fast and long-range weapons is not just inevitable, it is already unfolding, and the proliferation of the hypersonic weapons, if one considers the dynamics of the increase in their range, will, in the event of conflict, close off large coastal areas of Eurasia for the U.S. Navy's surface fleet.

The ominous announcement that Russia is getting ready to deploy a lighter version of her deadly *3M22 Zircon* hypersonic missile, which will allow it to be deployed on any combatant, should have attracted attention.[17] It did not. The ramifications of this, however, are immense since this missile allows even small missile boats to launch Mach=9 long-range anti-shipping (and land-attack) missiles. This opens the door, eventually, for hypersonic weapons proliferating into the wider world and eventually becoming a mainstay of attack weapons. Discussing a possibility of removing the U.S. Navy's carrier battle groups from the South China Sea by means of sinking them, a hawkish PLAN's Rear-Admiral Lou Yuan didn't mince words when stating on December 20 to the 2018 Military Industry List summit that China's new and highly capable anti-ship ballistic and cruise missiles were more than capable of hitting U.S. carriers, despite their being at the center of a "bubble" of defensive escorts. He also observed: "What the United States fears the most is taking casualties."[18] While controversial and belligerent, Lou's words certainly indicated a serious strategic and force structure problem for the United States and its Navy as its most important political and military tool. In peer-to-peer confrontation the U.S. Navy would face a salvo of high supersonic and hypersonic weapons and the U.S. simply doesn't have weapons able to stop it. The mathematics for survival is simply not there.

Some American professionals have reacted bitterly and harshly to Lou's declarations. The usually rational James Holmes of the U.S. Naval War College responded in a very emotional manner and listed some inapplicable lessons of U.S. carrier operations of WW II and even made a rather dubious argument:

A carrier is a big ship. It is tiny by comparison with the ocean, and can exploit being the veritable needle in a haystack. For instance, if a carrier group stringently regulates its electromagnetic emissions the way we cold warriors did—deploying a technique known as EMCON, for "emissions control"—it can limit if not entirely avoid giving away telltale clues to its location.[19]

It is surprising that James Holmes, who is J. C. Wylie Chair of Maritime Strategy at the U.S. Naval War College, has completely forgotten that we all now live in the year 2019, not 1970 or even 1985. Modern over-the-horizon radars allow the detection and tracking of surface targets many hundreds of kilometers away, and both Russia and China have these capabilities. Modern reconnaissance-targeting satellite systems (constellations), such as Russia's *Liana,* provide reliable targeting against surface, ocean and ground threats, especially against such massive targets as aircraft carriers.

In the end, a fishing boat spotting a carrier battle group and giving its own position and bearing and range to that carrier provides more than enough targeting data for modern supersonic and hypersonic weapons which are capable of final refined reconnaissance and target selection and re-distribution within the salvo. In a real war any fishing or commercial boat or vessel becomes a reconnaissance asset, a node in the network, capable of relaying information to other nodes, including higher-up ones, using a variety of radio, optic and other means. Nor should anyone discount, in case of real war, good old flag and light semaphore either. Not to speak of basic methods of navigation at sea, topography, orientation on the ground and other basic combat skills which atrophy very fast and did so long ago, such as the

over-reliance on GPS navigation by the U.S. Navy, resulting in the elimination of the position of navigation officer,
which, in the end, resulted instead in embarrassing collisions
for U.S. Navy ships. In the case of the Norwegian Navy, the
lack of fundamental navigation and maneuvering skills of
its officers resulted in the loss of an entire frigate, the *Helge
Ingstad*—5,200 tons of expensive military technology which
proved to be worthless in the hands of personnel who lacked
the basic skills required for watch and commanding officers
on the bridge.

And this is just the short list of challenges and revolutionary changes the United States faces today in warfare. The
main issue is whether U.S. policy makers can grasp the scale
of the problems the U.S. faces. There are so many reasons to
believe that they can't—they simply lack the required backgrounds in modern warfare to be able to grasp the real relation
between a nation's economy, its technology and weapons,
and its national security. Those people in the United States
who do grasp these issues—the majority of them are people
of military background—are either reluctant to speak out directly and on point about the United States basically losing
a conventional arms race, or are prevented from speaking
about it for ideological, political and, inevitably, security
reasons—both domestic and international—because it contradicts so dramatically America's self-image as boasting the
"finest fighting force in history" and exceptionalist historical
view of itself. Any assertion that there is, realistically, nothing "exceptional" about the United States' military is treated
as an anathema by the U.S. commentariat and punditry, leaving most of those people or their lap-dog "military experts"
to press on with bellicose delusional rhetoric.

It is understandable when people get upset, sometimes
emotionally justifiably, such as is the case of the verbal duel
between James Holmes and Lou Yuan, at seeing the object of

their love and admiration, to say nothing of the fruit and ballast of their professional life, fading from its former power and glory, but at least these professionals can formulate why this has happened once they are given the opportunity to think calmly. Sometimes, such professionals can even offer a way out—but this is not the case with American political and decision making class.

People with degrees and background in law, journalism or finance are not capable of independently forming competent opinions on military and, by implications, geopolitical matters, even if they try. Most of them have never experienced any serious life difficulties, such as hunger, sleep-deprivation, cold, or poverty, to say nothing of having served in uniform as military professionals—yet, these are precisely people in the U.S. who are most belligerent and ignorant in matters of war. American contemporary history is filled to overflowing with empirical evidence supporting this assertion. Studying Napoleonic Wars in detail can hardly help one understand how target-selection protocols operate in the homing devices of missiles, nor will the knowledge of the American Civil War explain how force is calculated and a combined arms operation is planned on the modern battlefield against a peer adversary. Those things are beyond the grasp of the contemporary American leadership. They simply do not understand numbers and how they apply to military and geopolitics. The only numbers they understand deal with approval ratings, stock options and largely fake Wall Street "economics."

Moreover, after the unprecedented U.S. internal political events of the last two and a half years known publicly as Russiagate and the de facto slow coup attempt against a legitimately elected U.S. President, however grossly flawed, to say nothing of the assault on the U.S. Constitution, no serious discussion addressing the psychological and psychiatric adequacy of the utterly corrupt American political class and its lap-dog media who completely discredited themselves is possible. Expecting from such an environment any sober assessment of the world outside, let alone such a complex issue as warfare, is simply an exercise in futility. It is impossible, as General Latif notes, to explain to people brought up on Hollywood version of warfare what operations in an EW dense environment against massive fire impact from the enemy are—the only type of warfare which will face the United States forces around the globe as time passes by and cutting edge technologies, both enablers and weapons, proliferate.

But even if these people "get it," a highly dubious assertion in itself, they will be forced by the imperatives of the American election cycle to repeat beaten to death and completely discredited clichés about American power. Without whipping up American jingoism and militarism, they will have no chance of being elected or selected to run by elites, whose interests largely contradict the interests of the majority of "deplorable" Americans who, in electing Donald Trump, supported a more cooperative, dramatically less interventionist foreign policy. As recent events have shown, the voice of the American people is worth nothing if it contradicts the desires of the moneyed and allegedly "smartest in the room" American classes. This America was cheated, yet again, both by the elites and by the new president himself, who ushered in an unprecedentedly militant foreign policy, including by means of bringing onboard his administration people such as the draft-dodger, serial liar and manipulator, John Bolton, who was too much even for George W. Bush's war-like administration.[20] The current Trump administration is saturated with people like John Bolton or convicted crook Elliot Abrams. As recent revelations suggest, Donald Trump, a man with zero crucial real national security experience, is being easily manipulated into the most dangerous decisions either by his utterly incompetent inner circle of relatives or by such people as his CIA director, Gina Haspel, who played a crucial role in Trump's slippery slope towards ruining Russian-American relations by presenting false information and appealing to emotion.[21]

No serious geopolitical player would view these demonstrable facts, among many numerous others, of the complete and well-documented collapse of the American statecraft and the evaporation of any residual, however miniscule, trustworthiness, as other than the indication of the across-the-board decline of American political and cultural institutions. All of them, without exception, demonstrate increasingly their internal rot and lack of any effectiveness, be that American "diplomacy" which long since ceased to have anything in common with the millennia-old art of diplomacy, or the economy, education or the military. And many no longer believe that anything constructive can be achieved in concert with the U.S. Speaking at the Arctic Forum in 2019, Russia's President Vladimir Putin, responding to the moderator's question about his being invited to the White House, replied with sarcasm, with a quote from *Golden Calf,* a novel widely popular in the former USSR, which effectively underscored Russia's lack of trust or any desire to talk to the present U.S. power elite.[22] Putin softened the sarcastic harshness of this quote somewhat when he added that the situation must ripen before any decisions are made, but his clarification did not in any way obscure the fact that Russia does not see the current United States as a negotiations-worthy party. This was just another in a string of top Russian officials and policy-makers giving up on the U.S. Foreign Minister Sergei Lavrov refused altogether to answer questions from a correspondent from the Washington Post at a recent Munich Conference, directly telling the American reporter to write whatever he wanted since, as Lavrov directly stated, it didn't matter what he answered, since the

American public wouldn't get his message, which would be either misrepresented or misquoted.[23] Lavrov was correct in pointing out a normal practice of the American media, which is increasingly becoming the laughing stock of the rest of the world, having long ago ceased reporting the news, having turned instead into crude propaganda instruments of various Washington power factions.

Yet, such attitudes by those proclaimed by U.S. media and power elites as America's "adversary" should worry them and they do. They do because Russia herself behaves as a superpower who has woken up from an internally induced coma and which has about had it, as have very many others, with Pax Americana which has turned out to be only good for spreading chaos, destruction and death around the globe. Such a behavior, American geopolitical and pop-military "academe" presumed, wasn't supposed to be and wouldn't be exhibited, but it is now a reality. The immediate instinct of a thinking person would have been to question one's own intellectual framework and the validity of the methods one used to draw wrong conclusions. This is not the case with the American powers that be.

Most of the American elites, at least for now, still reside in a state of Orwellian cognitive dissonance. This is nothing new for the contemporary West, which long ago started its earnest transition into the severe cognitive dissonances world where, per Orwell's *1984* depiction of same in a totalitarian state: war—is peace, economic decline—is economy boom, military defeat—is victory, countries calling for peace—are aggressors. In the end, Western in general, and American es-pecially, military-political scholarship and analysis, for the most part, are nothing more than yet another manifestation of a complete American epistemological collapse—most recent American theories and models, especially in warfare, do not work. In fact, they never did while the United States was enjoying an unprecedented growth in prosperity and stability resulting from the U.S. remaining the only major power standing intact after the devastation of the WW II. This era is over.

Even incredulous U.S. media begin to sound less assertive, admitting, through their teeth, that the U.S. is facing now two superpowers in Russia and China, that Russia's economy is not smaller than that of Texas and that China's real economy has been much larger than the American one for years. But most importantly, *the U.S. has to face the very real prospect of its forces sustaining a massive military defeat at Eurasia's periphery* in case someone in Washington decides to probe China and Russia's resolve to rearrange the colossal Eurasian economy in such a way as to allow peaceful co-existence and prosperity for all. In the end, it is not just the Chinese economy's size which matters here—it is the high probability of unacceptable losses by American forces in case of war on China or Russia, let alone in a suicidal scenario of the U.S. and NATO attacking both. This is not to mention the fact that both China, not to speak of Russia, have the capacity to destroy the United States proper. This new geopolitical state of affairs is already here and it became possible primarily because of the real Revolution in Military Affairs and primarily in conventional weaponry which blew the myth of American conventional invincibility out of the water. The U.S. needs to acknowledge this reality or it will be risking what I described in my previous book, *Losing Military Supremacy*—accidentally stumbling into a war against Russia or China which the U.S. cannot win conventionally, let alone through the nightmare of a global nuclear catastrophe.

But as much as new warfare paradigm is terrifying, with more and more deadly weapon systems already deployed or in the design phase, one has to be very clear not just on what is at stake, but on who will be calling the shots, when faced with this colossal question. As Ron Ridenour astutely observed in his aptly titled book, *The Russian Peace Threat,* "Trump did surround himself with Dr. Strangeloves."[24] That is a significant factor in the conflict. In keeping with what some absurdly call modern warfare "hybrid," let us recall one which should be regarded as one of its component features—the enemy also has a say. China and especially Russia have a very significant say in how the world can avoid a global war. It goes without saying that with the United States today this can be done only by means of outmatching it militarily, which also means by matching it scientifically, productively, and demonstrating moral superiority in deeds and ideas over its completely discredited and cheap utterly abused propaganda of "democracy" and "human rights." This entails the widespread recognition of a new definition of a good life which cannot be achieved until new world order emerges which accords recognition and operational reality to International Law. Such a good life cannot exist without Peace, as in the absence of war, with peace being the only irrevocable condition not just for a good life, but for life itself—and that is what, in a grim ironic historic twist, the real Revolution in Military Affairs is now capable of providing for our time. It can provide, across vast expanses, a gun at the temple of every single Dr. Strangelove who, as history testifies so clearly, have congregated primarily in the nation which has never experienced real war and its horrific consequences: the United States.

It is really remarkable how, far from abstract whiteboard economic theories, which have zero grounding in real life, or far from variety of power-ranking models, a few combat models—from the relatively simple such as the Salvo Model, to the much more complex augmented Lanchester modelling, to modern operational planning, can give a real insight into the geopolitical balance. They also provide the greatest analytical tools concerning economic, scientific, educational, and even social trends, by means of presenting the developmental factors of such weapons and their use in real life. After all, as I have held for decades, small and relatively backward economies simply cannot produce combat networks, hypersonic weapons, satellite constellations, advanced nuclear and diesel submarines, advanced radar and air-defense systems. Even the seemingly achievable task of creating a modern, truly effective and networked tank or combat vehicle is the prerogative of the number of nations which could be counted on the fingers of one hand.

Modern weapons and all that accompanies them, those proverbial enablers, continue to be, as they were for centuries, one of the most important measures of the true power of a nation and its ability to exert massive geopolitical influence. While for decades the United States positioned herself as untouchable in this sphere—a lot of it was bluff, sometimes utterly tasteless and easily recognized. This, however, never prevented the United States from constructing its own delusional universe, the exit from which can be extremely painful, but will happen one way or another. We will look at some possibilities that might have been taken by the West in general and the U.S. in particular in those times when their bluff was called.

CONCLUSION

A New Era Begins

It is a dramatic experience for a relative outsider to read a profound and, no doubt, arduously achieved conclusion from someone with such a personal history of service and sacrifice for the United States as the CIA's own Philip Giraldi. In a few words he described the state of the world today which remains beyond the grasp of so many in position of power in the United States.

> It is depressing to observe how the United States of America has become the evil empire. Having served in the United States Army during the Vietnam War and in the Central Intelligence Agency for the second half of the Cold War, I had an insider's viewpoint of how an essentially pragmatic national security policy was being transformed bit by bit into a bipartisan doctrine that featured as a *sine qua non* global dominance for Washington.[1]

In this dramatic statement, Giraldi expresses not only his personal opinion of the evolution of America's Evil Empire, but also speaks on behalf of a vast majority of the population of the Earth. In one of its polls in 2018 Gallup recorded a drop in the world's approval of the United States' global leadership to 30 percent, a number equaling that of China and Russia.[2] What Gallup missed is the fact that far from losing in the "global leadership" category, whatever that means in globalist newspeak, the U.S. is consistently perceived as the number one threat to the world peace. That is precisely what Gallup found out in late 2013 in one of its polls, where the United States won this dubious distinction with a huge lead over second place Pakistan.[3] Philip Giraldi, unlike John Mearsheimer, doesn't bother himself, and correctly not, with ideological chimeras such as Liberalism or the Good Life, he goes for the jugular, when describing U.S. legislators' hallucinations, bordering on mental breakdown, about the world beyond U.S. borders in general, and Russia in particular:

> The Senatorial commentary is, of course, greatly exaggerated and sometimes completely false regarding what is going on in the world, but it is revealing of how ignorant American legislators can be and often are. The Senators also ignore the fact that the designation of presumed Kremlin surrogate forces as "foreign terrorist organizations" is equivalent to a declaration of war against them by the U.S. military, while hypocritically calling Russia a state sponsor of terrorism is bad enough, as it is demonstrably untrue.[4]

These are the kind of people who steer U.S. foreign policy today and develop U.S. pipe dream military doctrines in which the United States is assumed to be a benevolent hegemon capable of spreading democracy globally, including by means of a sword which, allegedly, is unstoppable. These are, of course, patently false assumptions which lack, as is the case with most U.S. analytical organizations' conclusions, a realistic assessment of the U.S. role and capability, while simultaneously failing to acquire an understanding of that of America's designated enemies, such as Russia. American power elites are aggressive and come across as reckless precisely because they lack serious military or intelligence background and tools for developing awareness, albeit sometimes even if they were to hold a combination of both it would not prevent a complete lack of awareness.

It may, indeed, come as a shock for many U.S. legislators or moneyed exceptionalists to recognize the fact that the U.S. is, indeed, the main threat to global peace while what constitutes U.S. hard power, especially its military power, is not capable of ensuring the supremacy which remains fundamental to these people's belief systems.

Yet, viewing today's United States as an imperialist power, which it really is, one is inevitably pulled towards the more than one hundred years old prophetic definition of Imperialism by Vladimir Lenin who provided descriptions of its main properties in his 1916 treatise *Imperialism, The Highest Stage of Capitalism:*

1. the concentration of production and capital has developed to such a high stage that it has created monopolies which play a decisive role in economic life;

2. the merging of bank capital with industrial capital, and the creation, on the basis of this "finance capital," of a financial oligarchy;

3. the export of capital as distinguished from the export of commodities acquires exceptional importance;

4. the formation of international monopolist capitalist associations which share the world among themselves, and

5. the territorial division of the whole world among the biggest capitalist powers is completed.[5]

With some adjustments for technological development throughout 20th and 21st century one is struck by the accuracy of his description and its relevance to the state of modern day America. One doesn't have to be Marxist to appreciate the degree to which the United States fits the bill of an aggressive Empire, especially when one looks at both economic and military statistics of the last 20 or so years, which can no longer hide the distinct relation between U.S. aggressiveness and the decline of its power, be that economic, military or intellectual. While the driving forces behind such a state of affairs are complex, the origin of this crisis is not derived from different metaphysical views on a Good Life, it is a natural crisis of liberalism, or, speaking generally, of financial capitalism reaching, in Marxist lingo, its highest stage. The financialization of the American economy by the mid-2010s has reached an absurd scale and so mauled U.S. manufacturing that, Michael Collins described it:

> This is no longer the capitalism described by Adam Smith; it is financialization—defined as the "growing scale and profitability of the finance sector at the expense of the rest of the economy and the shrinking regulation of its rules and returns."[6]

Financialization and outsourcing, which are largely responsible for killing American manufacturing and with it large segments of American technological competence, is based on money-making for the benefit of shareholders whose interest is only in their return on investment, irrespective of the well-being of the nation. Because of that, crucial competencies and capabilities are being stripped from what remains of U.S. manufacturing, while capital gravitates to the fields which always guarantee a good return—the main one of which, apart from financial Ponzi schemes and real estate swindles, is America's Military-Industrial Complex. That means war—perpetual warfare—is the only Modus Operandi which can sustain the last vestiges of money-making for big investors in the United States. War thus becomes not just a manifestation of American Imperialism—it becomes the only way the United States economy can continue to operate currently and postpone the proverbial day of reckoning.

But this day is coming and American power elites are feverishly trying to ignite the fire of a global war, believing that the United States will be spared the death and destruction planned for lands other than America proper. This belief is both dangerous and utterly delusional, and most importantly—even mathematics, dispassionate as ever, no longer supports such a view. Rephrasing a saying attributed by many accounts to Viscount Turenne—"fortune was for the big battalions"[7] in a manner suitable for the 21st century—one can confidently say that *fortune is for the hypersonic weapons.* Of course, enablers matter too, but in the end, what really decides the issue is the capacity to deliver high explosives to a target in the most efficient, that is to say, with minimal losses, and in an accurate manner. Those who can do it better on the ground, at sea and in airspace and beyond, in a scenario of a classic military conflict between major powers—those will win the hot phase of a conventional war and will be able to dictate the conditions of peace, if there are survivors. The real Revolution in Military Affairs brought about by hypersonic weapons allows those who possess them to control the escalation and win the war.

This is a terrifying scenario but it is the result of a process which has been taking place for decades now—as precision guided stand-off conventional munitions gain the ability to have not only tactical or operational, but strategic impact equaling that of a nuclear weapon. In the end, it makes no difference in what way U.S. Navy's Carrier Battle Group(s) poised to attack Russia or China's assets will be destroyed. In the 1970s and 1980s such an undertaking against a single U.S. Navy CBG could have been accomplished by at least two regiments of the Soviet Navy's missile carrying aircraft and could have involved tactical nuclear weapons. Needless to say, in such a scenario, the probability of the survival of many of those Soviet aircraft would not have been very high. Today, the destruction of a naval force—as an example, that in the East Mediterranean— can be accomplished by a couple of TU-22M3(M) bombers and a squadron of MiG-31K carrying *Kinzhal* missiles with purely conventional warheads. All launches of *Kinzhals,* and possibly X-32 missiles, can be done well outside of the ranges of the weapons carried by the CBGs aircraft. During such an operation any hostile naval force will be operating in an extremely dense EW environment, having most of its communications jammed and such systems as GPS disabled completely or rendered useless. Modern Russian strategic communications jamming systems such as the Murmansk-BN are capable of completely disabling the main U.S. communication networks, such as the High Frequency Global Communications System—NATO's main communications tool—on distances of up to 5000 kilometers.[8] This is an unprecedented deterrent capability which does make a significant impression on at least some professionals in the Pentagon.

As U.S. Deputy Undersecretary of Defense David Trachtenberg noted, while speaking at the Brookings Institution on Nuclear Deterrence: "It takes two to race," and the United States is "not interested in matching the Russians system for system. The Russians are developing an incredible amount of new nuclear weapons systems" *and generally* "are doing a number of things we are simply not doing."[9] Trachtenberg, while repeating beaten-to-death propaganda clichés which are in the foundation of the American so-called defense strategies, did not exhibit even the remotest understanding, while claiming to the contrary, of the nature of the real Revolution in Military Affairs not the causalities

157

behind it. Trachtenberg's Orwellian newspeak, a discourse centered on aggressive capacity sprinkled with cognitively dissonant terms such as "deterrence," was a surreal reminder, considering Trachtenberg's important position in Pentagon, of the dangerous dysfunctionality of Americans' vision of their country's capacities in relation to the world outside. For a country, which since 1945 is responsible for millions of civilian deaths with entire nations and cultures destroyed, and which has unilaterally withdrawn from one arms limitations treaty after another, the 1972 ABM being one such crucial treaty, failing to recognize that the United States is the aggressor against which a deterrent, both nuclear and conventional, is not just needed but imperative, seems to underscore not only a loss of any morality but a complete loss of any awareness.

Trachtenberg's presentation is indicative of two major dysfunctionalities in the American military-political process:

If Trachtenberg knows the real state of affairs globally, as assumed by his immensely influential position as Undersecretary in charge of policy, his presentation can only be assessed as deliberate misinformation. This is dangerous, because it does influence public opinion, especially when done through an institution such as Brookings, known for its exceptionalist and interventionist views.

If, however, Trachtenberg sincerely believes in what he is talking about, and especially what he doesn't talk about, such as the U.S. being perceived as the greatest threat to peace, then this is even more dangerous since it reveals a complete intellectual collapse among not only the significant participants in the American public political process, but among people who are supposed to know better.

It appears they don't know better, as an unprecedented assault of Russiagate on what's left of the once proud Republic demonstrated. Even President Trump's recent calls on U.S., Russia and China to reduce nuclear arsenals is nothing more than crude PR and, remarkably, yet another sign of Washington D.C. living in a make-believe world, since China cannot even theoretically be party to such a reduction due to China's strategic nuclear arsenal being dwarfed by those of Russia and the United States. No involvement of China in such reductions is possible until Russia and the U.S. reduce their arsenals to levels comparable to that of China. How President Trump envisions such a reduction in practice remains one's wildest guess. Such calls designed primarily for show are expected from a man whose decisions on crucial geopolitical issues, such as Russian-American relations, can be emotionally influenced by the photographs of sick children and dead ducks presented to him by his own CIA Chief, Gina Haspel, in an attempt to frame Russia for the obvious false flag Skripal Affair.[10] The fact that the Skripal affair as a whole was a nothing more than Anglo-American secret services trying to frame Russia and had crude provocation and false-flag written all over it didn't matter. One is left guessing how such a decision-making Modus Operandi by the leader of a nuclear superpower must be viewed from Moscow or Beijing. Given the barrage of ever increasingly militant rhetoric emanating from the Trump Administration's very own cabal of neoconservatives, no one takes the U.S. seriously anymore as a party to any negotiations and many do expect things to get out of control, thus increasing dramatically the probability of a war initiated by the declining United States.

In its recent editorial, symptomatically titled *This Is the End: The 243 Trillion Dollar Bomb Was Placed under the Global Economy,* a reputable Russian news agency, *Ria,* gave a grim forecast for the global and, especially, American economy which the author of the article calls a Debt-generating Machine.[11] Russians are not the only ones pointing to the approaching catastrophe; no less an authority than the head of the International Monetary Fund, Christine Lagarde, warned of an impending financial crisis which is being precipitated due to massive debt.[12] Colonel Wilkerson went even further when he cited Congressional Budget Office's conclusions that if the present rates of payments, adjusted for inflation, on the national debt and of the increase in military spending by the U.S. remain the same, by 2030 the U.S. government will have *no* discretionary spending.[13] How likely is it that the American leadership will not see war as the only way to dissolve the immense economic, social, cultural and psychological pressures constantly building up within a neo-liberal globalist system no longer capable of supporting its main pillar and beneficiary—the United States.

Can the present U.S. power elites unleash such a war, which, theoretically may reset this debilitating American debt? After all, fanatics do run U.S. foreign policy today. If that wasn't bad enough, as the long act of major public institutional self-mutilation by the absurdity of Russiagate has demonstrated, U.S. elites in general are infantile. The infantilism and petulance of the whole system is manifested through the incessant lying and irrational behavior which became the norm at the American political Parnassus, in media and art. Lying also became the norm in the economic field, and especially military field. While the Soviet system, to which more and more parallels are being drawn in modern day America, was known for simply not reporting on issues which might otherwise have undermined it, modern day America is in a full blown alternative reality creation mode on such an unprecedented scale it would humble the moribund Soviet propaganda machine. As one of the most astute American thinkers of modern age, James Howard Kunstler, described it:

How to account for Americans being the most anxious, fearful, and stressed-out people among the supposedly advanced nations? Do we not live in the world's greatest democratic utopia where dreams come true? What if the dreaming part is actually driving us insane? What if we have engineered a society in which fantasy has so grotesquely over-run reality that coping with daily life is nearly impossible? What if an existence mediated by pixel screens large and small presents a virtual world more compelling than the real world and turns out to be a kind of contagious avoidance behavior—until reality is so fugitive that we can barely discern its colors and outlines beyond the screens?[14]

It is impossible for average Joe or Jane to cope with this reality anymore. The only way is escape into this very alternative reality, be that the dopamine intoxication of social networks, sports, increasingly degenerate art and reality TV, or in a much grimmer way—throwing one's life at the altar of drugs and anti-social behavior. Pink Floyd's great analogy of being comfortably numb applies like never before to American society. So much so, that some observers, distraught over the Western public's dormancy in the face of a possibly catastrophic global war, even go so far as to call out Vladimir Putin for not scaring Americans into wakefulness. This ironic quip by peace activist Gilbert Doctorow didn't mince words:

> That, my friends, is the reason I say Vladimir Putin has done his and our people a disservice by not engaging in public diplomacy with the American and European peoples, by not scaring us properly so that we can come to our wits and compel our politicians and media to do likewise.[15]

The fact that Vladimir Putin, being a responsible president of a nuclear superpower, never lowers himself to uttering empty threats, or making grandiose hollow statements not to mention belittling anyone, as is a norm in American domestic and foreign political discourse, is not, of course, a sign of weakness. On the contrary, it reflects a general national Russian attitude towards war, which is very restrained and realistic. The fact is, academic product in the contemporary Western, so-called Russian Studies field is reduced to a collection of clichés, banalities and outright lies, not conducive for properly interpreting Russia and her president's behavior. Many among the American and European peoples are simply removed from the reality of the massive global realignment, hardly surprising in an age when their mainstream political organizations, from local to national, are increasingly dormant, if not comatose, in relation to foreign affairs. They, however, should be scared especially when they consider who is running American foreign policy—as should the world. No person embodies both catastrophic incompetence and ignorant militancy, bordering on psychopathy, as current National Security Adviser to President Trump John Bolton.

Dexter Filkins, who wrote an extensive expose on Bolton, notes Bolton, a lawyer by education, is, for all intents and purposes, a draft dodger:

> Bolton has spent decades in federal bureaucracies, complaining often of hating every minute. He has written wistfully of a note that Goldwater sent to an offending colleague: "Dear Bill: I am pissed off." Though Bolton says that he has never written such a letter, he has established himself as a ferocious infighter—often working, either by design or by accident, against the grain of the place to which he's assigned.[16]

How such a man, who is also known to blatantly threaten people and their families because they disagree with his views and methods, in the same vein as Hillary Clinton experiencing satisfaction speaking about the death of Qaddafi, could end up advising a president who himself is completely unschooled with regard to any military or geopolitical issue is both flabbergasting and a sign of the incessant degradation of American power elites.[17] In the end as Filkins states:

> Some former officials believe that Bolton's insularity could be dangerous, particularly in a crisis, when various arms of the government and the military have to mount a quick and coordinated response. "It's chaos under Bolton," the former senior national-security official told me. "The national-security adviser is supposed to facilitate the President's directives and coordinate national policy among the various government agencies. That process has completely broken down." The official added, "Bolton hasn't set any priorities. No one knows what the policies are—what's important, what's less important. The head is not connected to the body." Principals' meetings—crucial gatherings involving the President, the Joint Chiefs of Staff, and the heads of intelligence agencies—have become rare. "I don't remember the last time there was a fucking principals' meeting," the official said.[18]

Having fanatics in power who have zero qualifications in foreign affairs or, especially, in modern warfare, is a recipe for disaster. The past twenty years are exhibit A demonstrating such incompetence and self-destructive fanaticism. But can the contemporary American (or European) elite produce a real statesman today? The answer is no. American and EU bureaucracies are saturated with lawyers, economists, journalists and political so-called scientists, not to speak of clueless celebrities, many of whom, blinded by their own gigantic egos and completely confused by newspeak narratives, do not have the faintest idea of what could be at stake in case of a conflagration between the U.S. and China, not to speak of Russia. Yet, with some few exceptions, this is the only human material which is available and which in fact was grown and honed in elite American universities for the purpose of taking the reins of power in the future—in the U.S. in particular, and in the West in general. Business or journalism degrees, however, are not a substitute for true statesmanship, nor can the lack of even residual human integrity serve as a defining criteria for entrance into the political elite—as it appears to do. Human integrity and decency matter and in the end it is this which guides true statesmen to balanced decisions in favor of the national interest. How can the U.S. national interest be served if the well-being of the United States as a country, or of her peoples, ceases to be an issue of concern or focus, as a result of her elites' egos, ambitions and ignorance?

People with integrity and understanding of the big picture do still exist but as the experience of the last two decades has shown, they have virtually zero chances of getting to the political top which is firmly in the pockets of the bankers, the military industrial complex, sector-dominating corporations, billionaires and foreign interests such as those of Israel or Saudi Arabia. The never-ending theater of the American election cycle which offers the naïve population only two choices between bad and very bad, that is between fast and slow dissolution of American culture, solves absolutely nothing. As Russiagate demonstrated, the will of the people, of those very many labeled as deplorables doesn't matter a bit and the real owners of America have no commitment to it; they are ready to go to any length, even if it means severe damage to, if not destruction of, the American state as it was known since its inception. Any rhetoric on democracy, civil liberties and human rights in today's America is nothing more than propaganda fodder by a national-security-warfare state—against other states it wishes to subjugate. No other options remain in the U.S. but exceptionalists and militarists.

As Daniel Larison grimly and cathartically concludes about both Bolton and Donald Trump, which may as well be applied to the whole American establishment:

> In order to believe that the U.S. won't take military action against one or more countries at some point in the next two years, we would have to believe that Bolton won't get his way when there is disagreement inside the administration about what to do. To date, Bolton has prevailed every time. The profile presents Trump as an "isolationist" who doesn't want to intervene abroad, but that isn't true. If Trump really were an "isolationist," he would never have appointed someone like Bolton, and he certainly wouldn't keep deferring to him on one issue after another. Bolton is able to get his way with Trump so often because he knows how to flatter the president and because Trump is a militarist who doesn't have a problem with Bolton's "bomb first and then keep bombing" approach to foreign policy. Above all, Trump's desire to appear "tough" makes him receptive to brain-dead, hard-line arguments.[19]

This is the sad and dangerous reality of today's America. American elites in general are the extension of the American dysfunctional neoliberal, that is to say, hyper-capitalist, economic system and of an exceptionalist delusional view of America and, by implication, of the world at large. Neither are true in any sense of the word nor do they work anymore, if they ever did. The combination of neoliberal economic views, for some reason defined as conservative, and of an ultra-liberal social order doesn't work. It cannot. Nor are U.S. elites capable of learning the lessons which must be learned. The fact that highly credentialed academic Stephen Walt proclaims that, "America isn't as powerful as it thinks it is," changes absolutely nothing when American power elites are not capable of recognizing even basic economic, not to mention complex military facts "on the ground."[20] The only hope is that the United States, due to its own hubris, will not drive itself into a situation where it will experience a humiliating event which will de jure formalize U.S. departure from the status the U.S. thinks it enjoys or will force it to lash out militarily with catastrophic consequences for itself and the world. In the case of attacking Russia and, to a certain degree, China, such a scenario is not impossible.

The outside world is not oblivious to what is going on in the United States. It is preparing, knowing full well that the American economic order is on the verge of a complete collapse and that a new, much more cooperative and rule-based economic and foreign relations model is being gestated within the Eurasian landmass. Such a model, still in its infancy, must be protected. Moscow, as one of two, the other being China, guarantors of survival of such a model, is keenly aware of the dynamics in Washington, as it is aware of the futility of any negotiations which would see Russia's legitimate security concerns, not to speak of those of Eurasia as a whole, be considered. Trump, being a militarist with an administration infested with exceptionalist fanatics, is not worth negotiating with, since no agreements can be concluded in principle with a nation which, for all intents and purposes, is no longer governable. Speaking to Russia's Federal Assembly in February 2019, and commenting on the U.S. unilaterally abandoning the INF Treaty, thus opening the road to deployment of American intermediate and close range missiles pointed at Russia, President Putin, in an unusually blunt statement, declared:

> Russia will be forced to create and deploy those types of weapons...against those regions from where we will face a direct threat, but also against those regions hosting the centers where decisions are taken on using those missile systems threatening us.[21]

It is obvious what Vladimir Putin was alluding to. The only decision centers capable of issuing the order to attack Russia are located not on the territory of Europe, many countries of which are American vassals with zero decision making power, but on American soil. Russia's military-technological and strategic 21st century leapfrogging, which brought about a real revolution in military affairs, was precisely about stripping the United States of its cloak of real and largely perceived invulnerability due to its geography and of its fanatic following of America's military mythology. And this revolution is only at the beginning, as Russia's latest large geopolitical moves attest. In some sense Russia started doing, in a timely and well calculated manner, what American thinkers of Paul Craig Roberts' scale were calling upon Russia (and China) to do for years—to take a grand stand against the United States and by so doing, change the world.[22]

The world has, or rather was, changed. This change started in earnest in 2014 when Russia returned Crimea to its Russian home and didn't allow the illegal and violent coup in Ukraine to consume the population of an historically Russian land. Russia also, by providing aid, didn't allow Kiev and the West's stooges to capture the young Donbas Republics of LDNR. The conflict in Syria followed, bringing about the display of some of Russia's military capability which created a full blown hysteria in the United States. Today, four and a half years since massive geopolitical realignment started, one can see some contours of the emerging future world order, the one in which the United States is not a hegemon but just another major power which must balance out its legitimate interests with those of other major powers.

1. The unipolar world is over. It has been over for some time. Today, in 2019, this is becoming clear, however slowly, even to those who have lived in denial for the last 5 years. The end of this world was and is, at the time of writing, unfolding in a front of everyone's eyes, even despite all the efforts of globalist propaganda, which is increasingly crude and ineffective, to prove otherwise. The old world and the alleged "order" it produced since 1991 is simply unsustainable.

2. American liberalism—a euphemism for imperialism and financial capitalism—simply ran its course. While the Yalta/Cold War 1.0 world was over the minute the Soviet Union collapsed and treasonous groups came to power in Russia, America may not collapse at all, if it avoids an all-out ethnic and cultural hot war between what remains of the largely white Christian population and different ethnic non-white groups vying for the control of the remaining American resources and its nuclear weapons. It is yet to be seen if the United States avoids such a war.

3. Insofar as the American version of capitalism is unsustainable it also leads to a larger metaphysical issue. A good life in the full meaning of the word cannot be good as long as "the pursuit of happiness" is defined only by consumerism and by the "values" of fringe elites which attack the moral fabric of the overwhelming majority in a society. The United States is being subjected to incessant propaganda promoting bizarre lifestyles and esoteric pseudo-scientific concepts of matters ranging from education to art to sex, and admits but obscures the real injustice of its radical social stratification—

the proverbial split between the 1 and 99 percenters. No happiness can be pursued in the society where the whole cultural milieu is nothing more than an exhibit A of sexual, gender, drug, crime and economic dysfunction being promoted as a norm. Moreover, this agenda becomes a totalitarian noose which strangles the remaining liberties in America. But this is American society today and this is precisely the kind of society which cannot compete anymore with cultures which are based on millennia of historic experiences which allowed those cultures to survive and propagate.

Robert W. Merry, while trying to conduct sustainability tests for the current United States, noted:

> The sustainability test helps us understand serious underlying realities of America and the world in these turbulent times. Once it is applied (and I have applied it only to the most obvious cases), two questions emerge: Is America a stable polity? And is this a stable world? The questions answer themselves.[23]

America today is an unstable polity and unstable polities of the American scale still massive in economic and military terms, tend to unleash wars. After all, from Yugoslavia, Iraq and Afghanistan, to Syria, Libya, Ukraine and Venezuela—the American record of aggression and violent overthrows of legitimate governments in the last 20 years is simply stunning. Adding here a coup in Iran, the slaughterhouse of Vietnam, Laos, operations in Nicaragua or Panama to that list of American post WW II actions—one can only see a trail of destruction, suffering, refugee camps and death on the industrial scale. This is not a good record to contemplate with all the talk about a good life. Seeing this record, one is forced to the conclusion that for others, to survive and to lead any life, let alone a good one, one must get armed or find a guarantor of own security against a power which has

completely gone off the rails. Such a power did emerge, or, more precisely, re-emerged as of lately and so did weapons which changed geopolitical calculus. What once was beyond the grasp of so many geopolitical players of lesser scales, who wanted some guarantees of peaceful existence, suddenly appeared within reach—real military capability.

It goes without saying that the appearance of the Russian military anywhere in the world, as is the case with Syria, limits dramatically any military options for the United States (or Israel), to say nothing of the West's supported proxies, many of them outright terrorists, who begin to be annihilated by the Russian weapons which begin to flow to legitimate governments or by the Russian military itself. It is beyond any argument that Russia's interference in Syria saved this nation from becoming a nightmarish playground of the Islamic fanatics, and ensured Syria's existence as a secular Arab republic—a fact Israel will now have to face. In the Ukrainian conflict it was Russian EW and CISR capabilities, modern tactics, operational art and weapons, which allowed the outnumbered Donbas rebels to fight the large Ukrainian Army, first to a standstill and then, in a couple of brilliant moves, encircle and destroy large forces of the criminal Kiev junta, supported by the combined West, in a display of a vast operational advantage due to ably controlled and commanded forces, even despite being outnumbered, demonstrating what can be attained when there is a clear understanding of the political objective of the war leading to an extremely high morale within the resistance. The appearance of Russian military advisers in Venezuela in and of itself sent a clear message to the United States that Russia, despite vast distances, is not going to let Venezuela, however dysfunctional but having legitimately elected its government, to fall to a cabal of America-trained and financed stooges.

The map of the American geopolitical retreat—of the areas where America is no longer able to use indiscriminate force, as was the case until recently—is vast and it stretches across the whole globe. Yes, the United States still can send several Carrier Battle Groups in a futile attempt to intimidate North Korea, as an example. But North Korea fails to be intimidated and turns to Russia as a guarantor of North Korea's security. China is not intimidated at all and continues her massive, however doctrinally debatable, naval buildup. This is the effect of American militarism today— many simply take actions of one kind or another and they are arming. Two years ago, Andrei Raevsky, known to many over the alternative internet as The Saker, wrote a prophetic piece titled *The End of "Wars on the Cheap" for the United States*. In it Raevsky arrived at a crucial conclusion which in different forms has been circulating since around 2008 when Michael Saakashvili's military provocation resulted in the decimation of the Georgian Army and naval forces and the partition of Georgia. Raevsky notes:

> The Anglo Zionists have been punching above their real weight for decades now and the world is beginning to realize this. Prevailing against Iran or the DPRK is clearly beyond the actual U.S. military capabilities. As for attacking Russia or China—that would be suicidal. Which leaves the Ukraine. I suppose the U.S. might send some weapons to the junta in Kiev and organize some training camps in the western Ukraine. But that's about it. None of that will make any real difference anyway (except aggravating the Russians even more, of course). The era of "wars on the cheap" is over and the world is becoming a very different place than it used to be. The USA will have to adapt to this

reality, at least if it wants to retain some level of credibility, but right now it does not appear that anybody in Washington D.C....is willing to admit this. As a result, the era of major U.S. military interventions might well be coming to an end, even if there will always be some Grenada or Panama size country to triumphantly beat up, if needed.[24]

After Vladimir Putin's historic speech to Russia's Federal Assembly on March 1, 2018, I wrote:

The United States simply has no resources, other than turning on the printing presses and completely bankrupting itself in the process, with which to counter Russia. But here is the point: Russians know this and Putin's speech was not about directly threatening the U.S. which, for all intents and purposes, is simply defenseless against the plethora of Russia's hypersonic weapons. Russia does not have the objective of destroying the United States. Russia's actions are dictated by only one cause—the equivalent of pulling a gun on a drunk, rowdy, knife-wielding bully in the bar and get him to pay attention to the ramifications and personal dangers of his actions. It seems that this is the only way to deal with the United States today.[25]

It was a real Revolution in Military Affairs which Russia started by producing and deploying weapon systems which denied the United States any ability to conduct "wars on the cheap." Today, any appearance of S-300 or S-400 systems, a plethora of supersonic and hypersonic weapons, of SU-30 or SU-35 fighters, not to speak of the upcoming SU-57 advanced aircraft, among many other systems, give even a middle-sized nation a chance against the possible attack by the United States by making such an attack enormously costly, thus providing a long needed deterrent effect against that country whose ignorant and aggressive elites claimed, due to their hubris and arrogance, that they had the right to decide its fate. Unless they want to unleash a nuclear holocaust in which the United States will assuredly be annihilated, the era of American militarism and imperialism is over, though we are yet to see, albeit it is now ensured, a final American departure from its self-proclaimed position of hegemon. In a bizarre and dark historic irony—today it is these, the most advanced and deadliest weapons ever produced in the history of humanity, which will allow keeping the peace on Earth, and with it, guarantee humanity's survival. Russia and Russians are keenly aware of that struggle they face. They have a poetic destiny of immense power.

Soviet poet Alexandr Trvardovsky left a Great Patriotic War literary masterpiece for the Soviet people—the epic *Vasily Tyorkin,* large and written in many self-contained parts, because many Red Army soldiers could never expect to read the entirety because of the possibility of being killed at the front. It was a poem about life and the combat of a simple Russian soldier, Vasily Tyorkin, which later transcended its literary origin and lived on in Russian folklore and culture. One of the most powerful episodes in Tvardovsky's masterpiece about *River-Crossing* under enemy's fire, encapsulates the meaning of the titanic struggle against Nazi evil:

> Бой идет святой и правый.
> Смертный бой не ради славы,
> Ради жизни на земле.
>
> The battle goes on, holy and righteous
> A deadly battle not for glory
> For life on Earth.[26]

Today, the same titanic battle for life on Earth is being waged globally for a new, better, freer, more just and more peaceful global order to emerge. This struggle is not for glory and the sword for forestalling evil has been forged.

doubtful this will happen as author seems blind to "dark state = control" criminal elites

Global –

Davos

(could 1984) The Great Reset

4th industrial revolution

Biological warfare

5G ☺? Global

transhuman neural interface and control grid.

What Is the Future of Warfare?

As was already established, models do fail and so do predictions. Nowhere do predictions fail more than in the field of warfare and geopolitics. Yet, the field of military forecasting and futurology is quite diverse and vibrant, and once in a while cogent arguments and forecasts, which fairly accurately predict the future of warfare—and by implication, of the global power balance—are made. It is worth repeating that modern geopolitics is the obverse side of military power and retains fairly little in common with the geopolitical ideas of Halford Mackinder expressed in his seminal "The Geographical Pivot of History." In the end, geography today is merely a backdrop against which the industrial, technological and military races unfold, with most of modern weapon systems having little difficulty in overcoming geography by virtue of their ability to cover gigantic distances in a very short time, while many of their enablers, such as satellite constellations, are located altogether beyond Earth's geography—in space.

In this sense, modern geopolitics is defined today not only by the well-known terms of Rimland or Heartland, among many others, but by the ranges of weapons designed precisely for overcoming the limitations geography imposes on a nation's activities, and their probabilities of hitting designated targets. It is also defined by the proliferation of such weapon systems. The ability to hit a designated target in a conventional, non-nuclear paradigm has changed the entire geopolitical calculus in a revolutionary way, including, in the case of the United States, what used to be viewed as strength rather than weakness—geographic insularity and military bases spread around the globe, thus violating a crucial military truism of concentration of force. America's military posture is an imperial one, and in modern circumstances that increasingly makes the U.S. military vulnerable. Today, all American military bases around the world are fully within reach by conventional weapons, to say nothing of nuclear ones, that can be launched from within Russian and, to some extent, Chinese territories.

Few would have predicted even 10 year ago that in case of war Russia could launch a salvo of cruise missiles such as X-101 at the U.S. base at Diego Garcia from within the safe air space of the Caspian Sea or Northern Iran. Today it is a given. The very notion of Iran being capable of deploying a wide range of guided missiles near the shores of Persian Gulf, thus making any operation against Iran even by the mighty United States Navy very risky, demonstrates this startling contrast between the geopolitical approaches of the early 20th century, when the geographic features of Persian Gulf and Iran would mostly dominate the imagination of military planners set on attacking Iran, with today's reality which is dominated by the ranges of Iranian anti-shipping missiles measured in hundreds of kilometers and the impact they can have on any operation against Iran, Iran's geography and terrain notwithstanding. In this particular case the Iranian C4ISR and her missiles guidance and active radar and optronic homing are by far the most important determinants, more than, however favorable for Iran's defense against land invasion, its terrain. Modern military geography today is defined primarily by technical capability, with terrain, or in a larger sense, geography still remaining an important factor, but less so. So, few predictions for a successful attack on Iran could still be made with any acceptable degree of accuracy.

In terms of prediction for warfare enablers, no better example of successful forecasting exists than Admiral Cebrowski's vision of net-centric warfare, which today is a feature of any first-rate military. Obviously, development of computers, sensors and data links was and continues to be a never-ending process and some precursors of modern combat networking have been known since the 1940s. The appearance of the first analog computers during WW II, such as the British *Bombe,* after all, was due to the military need to break codes. So it's not that everything just happened at once. Behind every serious technological or operational breakthrough in the last hundred or so years there was usually a massive, laborious and even tedious effort by very many people and organizations. In this sense, Cebrowski's conclusions were based on a vast body of previous experiences with increasingly potent computers and sensors from which inputs were processed.

One, of course, may argue about the accuracy of Cebrowski and his colleagues' vision of the net centric warfare but combat networks are already here, they are now and they are an integral part of any modern military designed to fight on the modern battlefield against peer state actors. For people still enamored with the military's propensity to use abbreviations, it almost begs that we add another letter, N, for Networks, to the now well-established C4ISR (Command, Control, Computers, Communications, Intelligence, Surveillance, Reconnaissance). The new abbreviation could read C4NISR or C4RINS, if one wishes. But jokes aside, it was clear to military professionals that such, at that time seemingly sci-fi, capabilities as combat networks or swarms of drones, were not far away once the processing power of computers and reliability of radio-communications grew in leaps and bounds, as it has done.

Yet, today we all are facing a very foggy future in warfare. It is foggy because of simple mathematics—the number of new technologies, which could be used in weapons systems and enablers, grows tremendously every year, thus growing the number of ways those technologies could be arranged to produce new, revolutionary capabilities. It is the same middle school level math principle which allows for multiple arrangements of different compatible things. Today we have very many such compatible technologies which could be arranged as weapons systems and enablers. We have, in fact, an unprecedented number of ways technologies can be arranged in the military and civilian fields. This complicates predictions on the emergence of radically new capabilities in the mid- to long-term future. What about in the relatively short historic term? It suffices to take a look at hypersonic weapons.

The revolution in hypersonic weapons, for example, couldn't have been possible without the truly revolutionary development in materials, from metal alloys to composites, which allowed for hypersonic missiles and vehicles to survive the extreme heat generated during such a flight within the atmosphere. Advances in chemistry also made the appearance of the high impulse fuels possible. High impulse fuels allow modern missiles to accelerate to hypersonic speeds. Developments in nuclear technologies allowed the appearance of such deadly weapons as *Burevestnik* (*Petrel*) and *Poseidon*. While we are still years away from the development of actual combat lasers, there is very little doubt that we are already living in the laser weapons paradigm, with some of those laser systems, such as the *Peresvet* being already fully deployed and ready for combat. Moreover, Russia has already defined laser weapons as one of the pillars on which Russia's defense will continue to be built.[1]

The list of technologies which go into weapons today is gigantic, it dwarfs the even fairly recent—thirty or so years ago—list of technologies. For many lay people fascinated with the looks and the use of modern weapons as shown in modern media, the winding long road that many modern stand-off weapons took to reach the accuracy of a few feet may come as a surprise. Inertial navigation, or to be more precise, inertial dead-reckoning corrected through external positioning, is not new. It has been around since the 1940s, then being based around physical gyroscopes and acceler-ometers, and analog computers. Frequent positioning and introduction of the corrections was required to offset the detrimental physical properties of such electromechanical systems, among which the most serious drawback was the drift of gyroscopes, which introduced serious errors in the process of dead reckoning or inertial navigation. For sub-marines, which at first used primitive inertial navigation, surfacing to take a fix of their position by means of visual means (including by celestial bodies, let alone radar) was fraught with the danger of being detected and annihilated. Modern technology based on laser gyroscopes, with their miniscule errors, allowed a precise guidance for stand-off weapons, which can now reach an area with the target in it with very high accuracy and precision and, in many cases, can now do the final refined search by their own onboard radio and optical means to acquire the target for attack. New technologies also allow modern submarines to navigate by dead reckoning for much longer, even till very recent times.

Nor would the infantrymen of the 1980s recognize their peers of today. It's not just the look which has changed dramatically over decades with modern infantryman being literally wrapped in new materials, including those which reduce infrared signature. But beyond that, there's the fact of their being completely "plugged" into the combat network of their own squad or platoon and even further, into the higher combat networks of their company or brigade, enabling them not only to provide data on their own position or deliver a video feed, but also having sensors reporting on the modern warriors' health by providing data on their pulse and frequency and depth of breathing. We all are already in the presence of exoskeletons which allow a dramatic increase in the physical strength of a modern warrior, thus allowing for greater ammo loads and number of weapons to be carried into the battle. It also allows for easier evacuation of the wounded from the battlefield.

In a 2009 sci-fi flick, *Surrogates,* movie director Jonathan Mostow envisioned the U.S. Army fighting its battles in the nearest future by means of soldier-operators controlling their avatars (surrogates) on the battlefield from darkened halls, while lying on comfortable chairs, far away from the dangers of actual combat. The death, or rather, destruction of the surrogate merely meant for the soldier-operator the activation of another one, not unlike how it happens in computer games with a few computer shooter lives available for the player. If anyone thinks that we are not in this era, they should really check reality. The U.S. Army has been operating remote-controlled aerial vehicles capable of killing the enemy for more than a decade now, with combat drones, which are in fact the first appearance of sci-fi surrogates, already involved in numerous controversies, including blowing up peaceful weddings with a massive number of civilian casualties.[2] If that wasn't enough, this seemingly life-saving technology brought some serious ethical issues to the fore, among which were the protestations of actual combat veterans when the Pentagon decided to award the U.S. Army's drone operators with a newly created *Distinguished Warfare Medal,* which existed for only two months before being cancelled with zero personnel awarded.[3]

Indeed, killing today, remotely, has become a serious moral issue within what is defined today as counter-insurgency. The loss of real-life contact with a probable enemy, or with probable civilians in many cases, is what makes such killing questionable. In the end, the intelligence upon which killing is executed by remote aerial vehicles could be and often is wrong, thus endangering on many occasions the lives of innocent non-combatants. Often, when civilians are killed due to false intelligence and poor human judgement, it is simply brushed off as collateral damage. The situation, however, changes dramatically in a classic standing armies clash in which the Clausewitzian dictum of maximum exertion of force becomes valid and applicable, and both the political and the strategic objects of the war—the annihilation of the enemy force—become very clearly defined, due to the opposing forces themselves being clearly defined. The first real taste of the return of combined arms warfare in the new century really wasn't the criminal invasion of Iraq in 2003 insofar as the U.S. Army faced off against the barely combat-capable Iraqi Army. Rather, it was the 2008 Russian-Georgian War in which, by some bizarre assessments, the Georgian Army was viewed as the best in the former Soviet Union.[4] This delusion didn't last long. It was dispelled in five days—the exact duration of the Russian-Georgian War when combined arms warfare stormed back into relevance with a vengeance. Later this relevance was confirmed in the Donbass and in Syria, both of which saw some of the most intense fighting on the ground, with the support of a variety of means, from air power and naval assets to EW, which constitute a system of modern combined arms warfare actively involved in fighting.

It is, of course, very tempting to apply the experiences and lessons of the fighting in the Donbass and Syria to predictions for the future of warfare but here no magic predictions wand exists. One thing, however, remains unchanged. With the end of the American-style globalization, also known as *Pax Americana,* the rivalry of great powers is back with a vengeance. John Mearsheimer was certainly not entirely incorrect when stating that the

> cycle of violence will continue far into the new millennium. Hopes for peace will probably not be realized, because the great powers that shape the international system fear each other and compete for power as a result. Indeed, their ultimate aim is to gain a position of dominant power over others, because having dominant power is the best means to ensure one's own survival. Strength ensures safety, and the greatest strength is the greatest insurance of safety.[5]

Once one considers that the main source of violence and instability in the new millennium is the United States one can easily arrive at the conclusion that breaking this cycle of violence requires either defeating or deterring American military power. While the American decline is obvious and is accelerating with each passing year, the future of warfare, at least in the short to middle term, will continue to be defined primarily in terms of countering America's real and its very many mythical military capabilities by nation-states which are intent on not living by American rules. Thus, as the experiences of China and especially those of Russia show, any technological, operational and strategic concept conceived inside the American national security-warfare state will be offset either symmetrically or asymmetrically. Those developments will continue to be the main driver behind the present day real revolution in military affairs and its evolution into the future. That is, until the United States completes her historical cycle of military and economic decline and re-defines herself as another important great power constituting a newly emerging geopolitical reality, or it completely implodes into internal strife and departs, possibly for a very long time, from the ranks of major geopolitical actors.

Until then, one such field where the United States will be constantly challenged is in combined arms warfare which involves further development of the war between very large troop formations. Those formations are not likely to disappear from the scene—tank armies, large infantry formations in general, forces capable to conduct a major combined arms warfare against another nation-state or coalition of those will remain the most important deterrent against any unfriendly actions within the Eurasian land-mass. Large standing armies, superbly equipped, including with battlefield robotics and state-of-the-art fire power, are here to stay. Can we envision robotic soldiers, not unlike those portrayed in the *Surrogates* movie, deploying to the battlefield any time soon? Probably not, given the immense expense of even a single such robot. Yet, remotely controlled fighting is already here and swarms of drones, in the air, on the ground and over the ocean are already being deployed widely and will only grow in numbers and capability.

Considering the colossal, and largest, economic power and resources concentration on the Eurasian landmass, it is not difficult to predict that the United States will continue its attempts to destabilize and fracture the emerging common market there. This becomes especially important for the United States, before China addresses the vulnerability of her Indian Ocean SLOCs (Shipping Lanes of Communications) to the actions of the U.S. Navy by means of re-routing China's trade mostly through the land-lines or well defended Arctic Sea Route where friendly Russia and her Northern Fleet, aided by the largest and most advanced ice-breaker fleet in the world, can provide for safe passage.

The late admiral of the fleet of the Soviet Union, Sergei Gorshkov, at the peak of the Soviet naval development in late 1970s to mid-1980s, continued to stress his seemingly simple idea, first officially articulated in his 1976 treatise, *The Sea Power of the State,* that the modern (Soviet) navy must be balanced.[6] Gorshkov's idea of a balanced fleet was that of a navalist, who envisioned a modern navy capable of conducting global operations ranging from amphibious landings, to global anti-submarine warfare (ASW) operations, to nuclear deterrent. Yet, throughout Gorshkov's long tenure as Commander-in-Chief of the Soviet Navy, one platform above everything else remained dominant in his thinking— the submarine. Unsurprisingly, the 1968 *Time* magazine cover featured the image of Admiral Gorshkov superimposed on a submarine at the periscope depth. In addition to the Soviet Navy's impressive development of its surface fleet at that time, the USSR developed submarines at a break-neck speed and eventually equaled or surpassed the U.S. Navy's submarine forces not only in their quantity but in quality too. Even the U.S. Navy grudgingly admitted in 1988 that the project 971 (NATO *Akula*-class) nuclear submarine was the best in the world.[7]

Gorshkov knew, as do contemporary Russian naval commanders, that no balanced fleet is possible without a powerful submarine component. Even in the worst times of the post-Soviet collapse, with the Russian Navy's surface component rusting away and disintegrating in the 1990s, submarine development never stopped in Russia because submarine forces were and are still viewed as one of the major elements of national security. Submarines, apart from strategic missile submarines serving as a crucial pillar of the national nuclear deterrent, are indispensable in an ASW role. They are also a major factor in operations, both as a defender and otherwise, on the Shipping Lanes of Communications

(SLOC). This fact is important when considering what is emerging as a flash point—one of many—between China and the United States in the oceans, the Indian and Pacific Oceans, to be precise. There is very little doubt that any American administration, as recently demonstrated by Donald Trump's affection for the most extreme neoconservatives, such as John Bolton or Mike Pompeo, will pursue the most aggressive policies both in relation to Russia and China. This is today the nature of the American state, driven by its crusading spirit of exceptionalism and desperate vain desire not to allow the emergence of economic and military peers.

China long ago surpassed the U.S. economically. In terms of its naval development, however, some questions still remain as of today. There is little doubt that China's naval force, PLAN, is capable of supporting the Anti-Access/Area Denial (A2/AD) measures China must undertake to secure its homeland from attack from the sea. But considering China's immense economic weight and obvious necessity to ship goods especially using the Indian and Pacific Oceans' SLOCs one has to consider a distinct possibility, in case of a serious conflagration between China and the U.S., of the flow of goods and energy being cut by a belligerent U.S., which is already undertaking steps to bypass or overcome China's A2/AD zones.[8] Things get even more complicated for China in the Indian Ocean, at what is known as *Maritime Silk Road*—PLAN will need to face a powerful world-class U.S. submarine force in case of escalation. Even for all the institutional problems the U.S. Navy experiences today, it still remains a premier global naval force whose real might, however impressive visually, rests not just with its carriers but with its nuclear submarines. Here in the open ocean, the U.S. Navy holds an overwhelming advantage over PLAN. The advantage is not just in quantity, it is in quality and in vast operational experience. While justifiable discussion on the vulnerability of U.S. aircraft carriers to modern anti-shipping missiles continues unabated in the U.S., there is very little discussion on the need for a potent submarine component. The U.S. Navy today deploys an impressive submarine force which boasts cutting edge technologies in both quieting and detection on its latest subs. With U.S. regional allies this capability is even further increased, once one considers the submarine forces of Japan and Australia.

While diesel-electric or non-nuclear submarines of PLAN can play a crucial role in defense of China's littoral, operations in the open ocean require nuclear-powered submarines. China has problems with this particular type. While PLAN's program of building surface combatants is extremely impressive, nuclear submarines remain its Achilles heel. As one Russian naval analyst observed in July 2018, citing also the *U.S. Office of Naval Intelligence Report,* modern Chinese nuclear powered submarines even lag seriously behind American and Russian third generation nuclear submarines, such as project 671 RTM (NATO *Victor III*-class) in terms of quieting—a key, albeit not the only, tactical and technical characteristic of a submarine.[9] Nobody can predict when and if China will be able to match its nuclear submarines' capability, and a surface force required for support of their operations, with that of the U.S. Navy but it is obvious that this issue must be high on the priority list of Chinese strategists. A maxim from Admiral Gorshkov can help. The maxim is simple—you can't have a modern, powerful and balanced navy without a powerful nuclear submarine component armed with modern weapon systems.

Is naval conflict between China and the U.S. possible? This is not an idle question. Today many observers are concerned about the possibility of such a conflict erupting due to disputes in the East and South China Sea.[10] Considering the increased level of belligerence emanating from Washington, which also acts increasingly in an irrational manner, one cannot discount the possibility of some people self-indoctrinated with delusions of U.S. exceptionalism and pseudo-scientific concepts such as Thucydides Trap making a decision to get the U.S. drawn into conflict with China. This must be avoided by all means. Paradoxically, China's development of a world class nuclear submarine force may become one such measure. As of now, however, PLAN remains an unbalanced navy which faces stiff competition on the high seas. Reaching the quality level of the latest American or Russian nuclear submarines will require a highly focused effort which will be very expensive and will require serious systematization of the experience already accumulated by PLAN. Considering the scale of such an undertaking one shouldn't then be surprised that China also seeks alternatives to Indian Ocean SLOCs such as the *Ice Silk Road,* the name for the Northern Sea Route, where China will get a much more cooperative spirit from Russia who already has a fleet of conventional and nuclear icebreakers operating on this route and who has defensive infrastructure being built in Arctic for precisely maritime traffic and natural resources development reasons. As one observer noted: "As long as solid Russia-China relations exist, the future of the Ice Silk Road is bright."[11]

Considering the current highly positive dynamics of Russian-Chinese relations which could be termed as nearly allied, it is difficult to foresee any complications between Russia and China in the short to mid-term future. A combination of the strategic flexibility afforded by alternative trade routes such as the Northern Sea Route and of the proper balancing of the Chinese Navy through development of its submarine forces may prove a decisive factor in China, countering, with Russia's support, American efforts to arrest the emergence of a new truly multipolar world. Moreover, China, concurrently with Russia, does place an emphasis on the development of its own genuine hypersonic weapons, especially its anti-shipping missiles.[12] New weapon systems and operational concepts are a decisive factor in configuring safe lines of communication both in the ocean and inside the Eurasian landmass for an emerging common market.

Yet, while the United States can no longer deny the very real and massive threat that the new, 21st century global battlefield presents for the U.S. forces and is struggling to catch up, work on the design and procurement of ever newer weapons systems continues non-stop both in Russia and China. One such system is an effective defense against these very same hypersonic weapons. Vladimir Putin was explicit in defining the future when he stated to representatives of Russia's military-industrial complex that Russia must deploy anti-hypersonic defense before the hypersonic strike weapons appear in foreign arsenals.[13] Putin recognized that such weapons will appear in American arsenal inevitably. Judging by Putin's statement, very little doubt exists that Russia has a program of anti-hypersonic weapons defense in existence and, most likely, once one considers capabilities of Russian air and anti-missile systems and the state of laser weapons development, such a defense is not only possible but will be deployed in a fairly short time.

The United States, certainly, is trying to catch up in this field. At least that is what Pentagon's 2020 Budget Proposal indicates—with $2.6 billion planned for the development of hypersonic weaponry.[14] The Budget Proposal, of course, is filled with lingo describing futuristic strike and defense weapon systems, including, of course, lasers, Artificial Intelligence and other items which even in the early 2000s seemed the stuff of sci-fi novels or movies. Yet, in terms of hypersonic weapons, American development focuses primarily on what could be defined as a booster phase of a program lingering since mid-2000s Prompt Global Strike (PGS) which envisions a system similar to the Russian *Avangard* hypersonic glider. It is worth noting that so far, the United States has enjoyed a rather very limited success in its own hypersonic weapons development and still doesn't possess a genuine high supersonic, to say nothing of a genuine hypersonic long range, anti-shipping missile. These are the weapons which today define a domain where the United States still retains, however tenuous, advantage—the ocean. Anti-shipping hypersonic missiles with the ranges exceeding 1000 kilometers, or 2000 as is the case with *Kinzhal,* are redefining naval warfare away from the traditional American carrier-centric navy. It is not surprising, then, that the United States wants explicitly to negotiate limitations not only on Russia's strategic nuclear arsenal, such as its newest unlimited range RS-28 Sarmat intercontinental ballistic missile, but on the *Kinzhal* which in the view of the United States, in the words of U.S. Under Secretary of State Andrea Thompson, constitute a "new kind of strategic offensive arms for purposes of New START."[15] Thompson and the Department of State are being disingenuous—the *Kinzhal* is by no means a strategic weapon per a classic definition, and it is certainly not intercontinental, but it surely is a new defensive weapon designed specifically for containment of threats emanating primarily from the ocean and there is only one, very real, threat to Russia from this direction—it is the United States Navy and NATO's allied naval forces.

Thompson's proposing negotiations on the *Kinzhal* is akin to Russia demanding negotiations on the U.S. Navy's nuclear aircraft carriers—their number and capabilities—a no-go from their inception. Yet Thompson's statement is another sign of the growing realization in Washington of a widening military-technological gap that is not in U.S. favor and inevitably, of the collapse of an entire power projection doctrine. In this sense the *Kinzhal* does have a strategic impact since it is a reliable weapon offering primarily the capability of a conventional annihilation of the U.S. Navy's main striking force—its Carrier Battle Groups. It is obvious that Russia is not going to be discussing any such weapons under any auspices. Based on now traditionally wrong assessments of own advantages, the United States did pretty much the same when in 2002 it unilaterally abrogated the 1972 ABM Treaty—all despite Russia's legitimate requests and protestations. In the case of weapons of the *Kinzhal* class the United States has no legitimate case for complaint. In the end, even before deployment of the *Kinzhal,* Russia put in service the very deadly *Kh-32,* an almost Mach five capable 1000-kilometer range anti-shipping missile, which on its own was a game-changer for the U.S. Navy's surface combatants, aircraft carriers included.

In an abstract scenario of a conventional war of NATO against Russia the U.S. Navy will not be able to use its aircraft carriers at the ranges closer than 2,000 kilometers from Russia's shoreline, under the threat of losing them, thus rendering its main striking force useless. This is not a fact many people in the U.S. establishment can easily swallow—in the end the foundation of any sensible military policy is always a correct bet on those technologies which define and will define evolution, or, in our case, the real revolution of military warfare. In a layman's casino lingo—one has to know what color and number to bet on. Undeniable, any weapons system has a supply side element to it which, when rephrased to be applicable for warfare, can be stated as: just about any weapons system, even the most bizarre and ineffective, can still be used and, in fact, can have some influence on tactical and operational dimensions of a war. One doesn't need to go further for an example than the Nazi *Gustav,* also known as *Dora,* gun which, though monstrous in size, caliber and costs, turned out to be nothing more than a white elephant or combat curiosity with at best dubious combat efficiency and impact on the battle field which was dominated by armor, aviation and maneuver. The *Gustav* was nonetheless used, primarily on the Eastern Front, merely because it was available. As some military historians noted:

Gustav had cost 10 million Marks, and the price of the ammunition is unknown, but its only achievement seems to have been the demolition of a few Soviet and Polish defenses and one ammunition dump, which was hardly a great achievement for a weapon that had cost so much in effort and money. For propaganda, or for boosting morale, or for frightening an unsophisticated enemy, Gustav, and the other super-guns, may have had their uses, but as a cost effective weapon of war it was nevertheless a non-starter.[16]

But if super-guns such as British or American gigantic mortars, were promptly removed from service or were never used at all, plus were produced in very small numbers, the situation with the F-35 fighter or Littoral Combat Ships (LCS) is a perfect demonstration of a mindless production continuation of a weapon systems which exists since it exists, and, of course, for its commercial reasons, but not for actual deployment on the modern battlefield. LCS are not survivable against any force with long range supersonic anti-shipping missiles, while the only two openly proclaimed combat virtues of the F-35, its networking and low observability, are, at best, dubious advantages against the modern air-defense complexes, EW means and combat aviation of America's peers. These peers also use networks, low observability and supermaneuverable aircraft which outperform the F-35 by a significant margin, while themselves carrying a dizzying array of cutting edge sensors.[17] But even the F-35's grossly talked up low observability in the radio diapason of modern aircraft is becoming an obsolete technology against what became known as ROFAR (Radio-Optic Phased Array).[18]

So, what is the future of warfare, then? The answer may come as a surprise—this future lies in people, as it has in the past and does at present. While we may endlessly discuss the already deployed or future combat technologies, in this deadly mix of machines and people, people remain what, in the end, decides the outcome of the battle, and indeed, of the war. If humanity is to survive deep into this century without unleashing nuclear Armageddon, any conventional war between nation-states very well may degenerate into the attrition warfare. If one major power decides to invade another, it will be people with all their knowledge, skills, will, morale, culture and patriotism who will decide the issue against the aggressor, because the seat of the government is always on land and it is there where, in the end, the fate of warring sides is decided. In a duration of the last 70 years, the United States, with all her real and exaggerated military capability failed to win a war against any determined, not to mention determined and moderately competent and well-equipped, adversary even when seemingly having an overwhelming technological advantage.

In this case we may, very cautiously at that, assume that despite the increasingly volatile world we all live in, the will of the great powers will be primarily tested by the declining United States through non-military means: ideological, economic, propaganda and sabotage. Even the conventional, to say nothing of nuclear, warfare of today holds such destructive and well-aimed power that the United States increasingly finds itself unable to counter the modern and very real Revolution in Military Affairs. Once the veil of propaganda and myth is removed from America's military capacity, what lies revealed is a state which, even if retaining its current rates of expansion of military expenditures and of accumulating national debt, will by 2030 have no discretionary spending left.[19] This is no recipe for it staying in serious military competition, when the U.S. has to maintain an immensely expensive naval surface fleet which is useless against modern technology, or cannot develop a new main battle tank, or is forced to rely on older aircraft, such as the F-15X, in order to have a viable air force.

These are the signs of a declining power which, for all intents and purposes, has lost the arms race, despite maintaining an edifice of military superpower. The U.S. lost it because of its hubris, the source of its inability to look into the future and change with it. At the foundation of such inability is the fundamental systemic crises of liberalism and its most dangerous iteration of American version of globalism—a dystopia which didn't take into account the will of the different peoples on this planet to retain their own histories, cultures and outlook on the world. For that, many have been ready to work tirelessly and even die. Doing so, they created a reality in which Western aggression was checked and eventually will be turned back on itself. The will to do that has now been found, and that is what in the end decides the outcome of any war.

ENDNOTES

Introduction

1 John. J. Mearsheimer, *The Great Delusion: Liberal Dreams and International Realities* (Yale University Press, 2018), 28–29.

2 Daniel Larison, "Why the U.S. Fails to Understand Its Adversaries," *The American Conservative,* April 5, 2018.

3 Charles L. Glaser and Chaim Kaufmann, "What is the Offense-Defense Balance and Can We Measure It? (Offense, Defense, and International Politics)," *International Security* 22, no. 4 (Spring 1998), 44.

4 Mearsheimer, *Great Delusion,* 4.

5 Plato, *The Republic: A Socratic Dialogue* (Oregan Publishing, 2016), 105.

6 Mark Thompson, "Iran Dissent Costs Fallon His Job," *Time,* March 12, 2008.

Chapter 1

1 Francis P. Sempa, "How to Avoid the Thucydides Trap: The Missing Piece," *The Diplomat,* March 7, 2018, https://thediplomat. com/2018/03/how-to-avoid-the-thucydides-trap-the-missing-piece/.

2 "SEMPA, Francis P. 1959–", *Encyclopedia.com,* https://www. encyclopedia.com/arts/educational-magazines/sempa-francis-p-1959.

3 Thucydides, *The History of the Peloponnesian War* 1(1), http:// classics.mit.edu/Thucydides/pelopwar.1.first.html.

4 Alexey Tsvetkov, Ловушка для политолога ("The Trap for Political Scientist"), *Liberty,* November 12, 2015, http://old.inliberty.ru/ blog/2089-Lovushka-dlya-politologa.

5 Ibid.

6 *Avoiding the Trap: U.S. Strategy and Policy for Competing in the Asia-Pacific Beyond the Rebalance* (Strategic Studies Institute and U.S. Army War College Press, February 2018), xiv–xv.

7 "Principles of War," *Encyclopedia.com,* https://www.encyclopedia.com/history/encyclopedias-almanacs-transcripts-and-maps/principles-war.

8 Lester W. Grau and Charles K. Bartles, *The Russian Way of War: Force Structure, Tactics, and Modernization of the Russian Ground Forces* (Fort Leavenworth, Kansas: Foreign Military Studies Office, 2016), xv.

9 Anthony H. Cordesman, *Lessons of the Gulf War: 1990-1991* (Center for Strategic and International Studies, 2013), iv–vii.

10 Ibid., iv.

11 Ibid,. 10.

12 Ciaran McGrath, "World War 3: Hypersonic weapons pose real 'challenge' to world peace, says expert," *Express,* January 5, 2019, https://www.express.co.uk/news/world/1066693/world-war-3-hypersonic-weapons-challenge-world-peace-russia-china-vladimir-putin.

13 Robert H. Latiff, *Future War. Preparing for the New Global Battlefield* (New York: Alfred A. Knopf, 2017), 124.

14 Andrei Martyanov, *Losing Military Supremacy: The Myopia of American Strategic Planning* (Atlanta: Clarity Press, Inc., 2018), 9.

15 Latiff, 131.

16 Ibid.

17 Roger Thompson, *Lessons Not Learned: The U.S. Navy Status Quo Culture* (Naval Institute Press, 2007), 167.

Chapter 2

1 Samuel Huntington, *The Clash of Civilizations and the Remaking of World Order* (New York: Simon & Schuster Paperbacks, 2003), 81–82.

2 Michael Mathes, "How the Polls Got it So Wrong on Trump," *AFP,* November 9, 2016.

3 "Obama Says Western Sanctions Have Left Russia's Economy 'In Tatters,'" *Moscow Times,* January 21, 2015.

4 Paul Sonne, "What did Trump Mean When He Said the U.S. Missiles Heading for Syria are 'Smart'?" *Washington Post,* April 11, 2018.

5 Ibid.

6 Kimberley Amadeo, "China is the World's Largest Economy for the Third Year in a Row," *The Balance,* updated January 30, 2019, https://www.thebalance.com/world-s-largest-economy-3306044.

7 Jürgen Scheffran, "Calculated Security? Mathematical Modelling of Conflict and Cooperation," in Bernhelm Booss and Jens Hoyrup (Eds.), *Mathematics and War* (Birkhauser Basel, 2003), 393.

8 Ibid., 395.

9 Akaev, Korotaev, Malinetsky, Malkov (Eds.), Проекты и риски будущего: концепции, модели, инструменты, прогнозы (*Projects and Risks of the Future: Concepts, Models, Tools, Forecasts*) (Moscow: Krasand Publishing, 2017), 89.

10 Ibid., 91.

11 Ibid., 92.

12 All estimated data in the example for both U.S. and China is from *Tradingeconomics.com* and World Bank.

13 Adam Ni, "Why China is Trimming its Army," *The Diplomat,* July 15, 2017.

14 United States profile, *Observatory of Economic Complexity,* https://atlas.media.mit.edu/en/profile/country/usa/.

15 *Assessing and Strengthening the Manufacturing and Defense Industrial Base and Supply Chain Resiliency of the United States,* Report to President Donald J. Trump by the Interagency Task Force in Fulfillment of Executive Order 13806 (September, 2018), 91–93.

16 "United States GDP from Manufacturing," *Trading Economics,* https://tradingeconomics.com/united-states/gdp-from-manufacturing

17 Central Intelligence Agency, "China," *The World Factbook,* https://www.cia.gov/library/publications/resources/the-world-factbook/geos/ch.html.

18 United States Census Bureau, *Trade in Goods with China, 2018,* https://www.census.gov/foreign-trade/balance/c5700.html.

19 Bureau of Economic Analysis, *U.S. Department of Commerce Gross Domestic Product, Third Quarter 2018 (Third Estimate), Corporate Profits, Third Quarter 2018 (Revised Estimate),* 19.

20 "De-dollarization: Scholars on Why Russia Bought Quarter of World Yuan Reserves," *Sputnik International,* January 15, 2019.

21 International Monetary Fund, "Report for Selected Countries, China," *World Economic Outlook Base,* 2018, https://www.imf.org.

22 International Monetary Fund, "Report for Selected Countries, Russia," *World Economic Outlook Base,* 2018, https://www.imf.org.

23 Joshua Waddell, "Innovation and Other Things that Brief Well," *The Marine Corps Gazette* 101, no. 2 (February 2017).

24 Peter G. Peterson Foundation, *U.S. Defense Spending Compared to Other Countries,* May 7, 2018, https://www.pgpf.org/chart-archive/0053_defense-comparison.

Chapter 3

1 As was pointed in the previous chapter, the key element of the geopolitical status of a nation is:

$$X_M = 0.5X_{M1}[0.5(X_{M2} + X_{M3}) + X_{M4}]$$

where M1 is a Share of the nation in global military expenditures, M2 is a military potential of the nation's Army, M3 is a military potential of nation's Navy and M4 is a potential of a strategic nuclear forces.

2 Congressional Research Service, *Navy Columbia Class (Ohio Replacement) Ballistic Missile Submarine (SSBN[X]) Program: Background and Issues for Congress,* Ronald O'Rourke, August 18, 2016, 10.

3 Congressional Budget Office, *Long-Term Implications of the 2019 Future Years Defense Program,* February 13, 2019, 1.

4 Joseph C. Harsch, "Who Has the Best Navy?" *Christian Science Monitor,* December 28, 1976.

5 See *supra* note 1.

6 Akaev, Korotaev, Malinetsky, and Malkov (Eds.), Проекты и риски будущего: концепции, модели, инструменты, прогнозы (*Projects and Risks of the Future: Concepts, Models, Tools, Forecasts*) (Moscow: Krasand Publishing, 2017), 102.

7 N.V. Mityukov, Определение Жертв Войн Через Ланчестерские Модели ("Estimation of the Victims of Wars through Lanchester Models"), *Historical Psychology and Sociology of History,* February 2009, 122.

8 This equation is in the foundation of what became known as

Quadratic Law:

$$(B_{start}^2 - B_{end}^2) = (A_{start}^2 - A_{end}^2)$$

To illustrate: We know that our B_{start} =750, we also know that our B_{end} –0, our A_{start} is 1000 and A_{end} is unknown and we will call it X. Look now at what our equation has become:

$$750^2 - 0^2 = 1000^2 - X^2$$

From here you can easily establish that the value of X, which is the number of remaining riflemen in the *force A* after they annihilate whole *force B* will be the square root of $1,000,000 - 562,500 = 437,500$ which is approximately *661* riflemen. That is 2.5 times more than linear approach would suggest. But this was very basic form of Lanchester's equations. In more advanced form those will look like this:

$$\begin{cases} \frac{dA}{dt} = -\beta B \\ \frac{dB}{dt} = -\alpha A \end{cases}$$

where Alpha (α) and Beta (β) are numerical coefficients which stand for attrition rates when accounted for combat effectiveness of opposing forces. Imagine if we were to overview a combat engagement between numerically equal forces but with one force having combat efficiency twice larger than the other. Let's utilize familiar to us forces A and B and say they equal 1000 each, while *force A* is twice better than *force B*, meaning $\beta = 1$, while $\alpha = 2$.

$$1000^2 - 0^2 = 2(1000^2 - X^2)$$

Force A will retain a square root of 500, 000, which is around 707 riflemen, as a result of its better combat efficiency, or quality, due to better weapons, training and organization. In fact, one can figure out how this quadratic, hence non-linear, relation works for forces which have a dramatic gap in their training, weapons and organization. One can grasp then why Russian, American or British Special Forces are feared so much. Such forces fight most of the time having much smaller numbers than their enemies but compensating for that by other combat factors which often allow them to come out victorious in many engagements with numerically superior adversaries. One can experiment with numbers when considering some abstract special operations force with $\alpha = 4$, while numbering 40 members against 180 regular militia.

$$180^2 - 0^2 = 4(40^2 - X^2)$$

You will get a negative number as a solution in this case and there are no real solutions for a square root of a negative number. In this particular instance it means the defeat of a special operations force, which needs to be either much larger, more than 90 fighters strong, to annihilate a militia while losing most of its fighters, or have better training, or additional firepower, which will increase special forces' α and ensure that it is not them, but the militia, who are annihilated.

9 Ibid., 11–12.

10 David M. Glantz and Jonathan M. House, *When Titans Clashed: How the Red Army Stopped Hitler* (Lawrence, Kansas: University Press of Kansas, 2015), 393–394, Table Q.

11 Yuri Bogdanov, "To Defend against NATO Larger Formations are Needed," *VZ.RU,* May 4, 2016.

12 Hon. James N. Miller (prepared statement), U.S. Congress, Senate, Committee on Armed Services, *Nuclear Posture Review,* 111th Cong., 2d sess., April 22, 2010, 7.

13 Yuri Solomonov, Америка предложит миру отказаться от ядерного оружия ("America will propose to the world to reject nuclear weapons"), *Altapress,* October 3, 2008, http://altapress.ru/obrazovanie/ story/ yuriy-solomonov-amerika-predlozhit-miru-otkazatsya-ot-yadernogo-oruzhiya-36578.

14 Office of the Secretary of Defense, U.S. Department of Defense, "Executive Summary," *Nuclear Posture Review,* February 2018, v.

15 Andrei Martyanov, "The Implications of Russia's New Weapon Systems," *UNZ.com,* March 5, 2018, http://www.unz.com/article/ the-implications-of-russias-new-weapons/.

16 Wayne P. Hughes, *Fleet Tactics and Coastal Combat* (Annapolis, Maryland: Naval Institute Press, 2000), 268.

The ΔA and ΔB system of equations looks like this:

$$\Delta B = \frac{\alpha A - b_3 B}{b_1}$$

$$\Delta A = \frac{\beta B - a_3 A}{a_1}$$

where a_1 and b_1 are staying powers of respective opposing ships, which is the number of the missiles required to take out of action those respective ships. a_3 and b_3 denote a defensive power of the opposing forces, which is the number of good enemy shots which will be destroyed or deflected by the defender. Alpha (α) and Beta (β) denote the striking power of each opponent, which is the number of missiles which would hit the target if there were no defense. A and B are the respective number of ships on each side.

17 Ibid.,1.

18 David M. Glantz and Jonathan M. House, *The Battle of Kursk* (Lawrence, Kansas: University Press of Kansas, 1999), 42.

19 Ibid., 280–281.

20 Michael Peck, "The Air Force Has a Plan to Save Navy Warships from Missile Attacks," *The National Interest,* January 10, 2019.

21 Vladimir Karnozov, "Putin Reveals Zircon Mach 9 Missile Specification," *AIN Online,* February 22, 2019, https://www.ainonline.com/aviation-news/defense/2019-02-22/putin-reveals-zircon-mach-9-missile-specification.

22 Wayne P. Hughes, *Fleet Tactics and Coastal Combat,* 289.

23 Раскрыта возможность перехвата "Циркона" ("The Probability of Zircon's Intercept is Disclosed"), *VPK News,* February 27, 2019, https://vpk.name/news/253802_raskryita_vozmozhnost_perehvata_cirkona.html.

24 Khvosh V.A. Voenizdat, Тактика подводных лодок (*Submarine Tactics*) (Moscow, 1989), Ch. 5.3.

The formula for a probability of a hit by a group of submarines on a surface target, which also accounts for a countermeasures from surface combatant(s) is next:

$$W_N = 1 - \left\{ 1 - P_S \left[1 - (1 - \frac{P Q_{(n)} Q_{tech}}{\omega})^n \right] \right\}^N$$

where:

P is a probability of a missile hitting a target;

n is a number of missiles in salvo by a single carrier (submarine);

$Q_{(n)}$ is a probability of each missile not being intercepted or seduced by countermeasures of the enemy;

Q_{tech} is technical reliability of missiles in salvo;

N is a total number of carriers (submarines) launching missiles;

P_S is a probability of each submarine retaining, due to enemy's countermeasures, its ability to launch a salvo;

ω is an average number of missiles required for a hard kill of a target.

Chapter 4

1 Matthew Mowthorpe, "The Revolution in Military Affairs (RMA): The United States, Russian and Chinese Views," *The Journal of Social, Political, and Economic Studies,* Summer 2005.

2 Ibid.

3 William E. Odom, "Soviet Military Doctrine," *Foreign Affairs,* Winter 1988/89, 120–121.

4 Andrew F. Krepinevich, "Cavalry to Computer: The Pattern of Military Revolutions," *The National Interest,* September 1, 1994.

5 Center for Strategic and Budgetary Assessments, *The Likely Future Course of the Revolution in Military Affairs,* December 2010, 5–6.

6 Steven Metz and James Kievit, *Strategy and the Revolution in Military Affairs: From Theory to Policy* (1995), 20.

7 "Israel's Deployment of Nuclear Missiles on Subs from Germany," *Spiegel Online,* June 4, 2012, http://www.spiegel.de/ international/world/israel-deploys-nuclear-weapons-on-german-built-submarines-a-836784.html.

8 Nedra Pickler, "Obama sends military aid to Egypt frozen after government overthrow, cites national security," *U.S. News and World Report,* March 31, 2015.

9 Netherlands Ministry of Defense, *2018 Defense White Paper,* 18.

10 Carl Von Clausewitz, *On War* (Princeton, NJ: Princeton University Press, 1976), 75.

11 Vice Admiral Arthur K. Cebrowski, USN, and John H. Garstka, "Network-Centric Warfare: Its Origin and Future," USNI *Proceedings* 124/1/1,139 (January 1998).

12 Norman Friedman, *Network-Centric Warfare: How Navies Learned to Fight Smarter Through Three World Wars* (Annapolis, Maryland: Naval Institute Press, 2009), ix.

13 David S. Alberts, John J. Garstka, and Frederick P. Stein, *Network Centric Warfare: Developing and Leveraging Information Superiority* (DoD C4ISR Cooperative Research Program, 1999), 251.

14 Robert H. Latiff, *Future War. Preparing For the New Global Battlefield* (New York: Alfred A. Knopf, 2017), 26.
Latiff presents Ignatius' view that "The U.S. has obviously concluded, not surprisingly, that the best strategy is to leverage its

biggest advantage, which is technology. The concepts are reminiscent of President Reagan's 'Star Wars' initiative, but thirty years on." It is difficult to see how evolution of weapon design along the lines of net-centric capabilities is related to Star Wars since very advanced for its time net-centric principles have been realized in late 1970s in MiG-31 interceptor. From the onset MiG-31 was capable to both interact and provide and receive targeting in a group of fighters, with A-50 AWACS and provide targeting for ground air-defense complexes. See, https://vpk-news.ru/articles/15752 | https://rg.ru/2014/02/03/mig-site.html.

15 Constantin Danilov, Непревзойденное Оружие ("Unsurpassed Weapon"), АО «ВПК «НПО машиностроения», http://www.npomash.ru/press/ru/podrobnee190713.htm.

16 David S. Alberts, et al., *Network Centric Warfare,* 91–92.

17 Sergey Sukhankin, "The S-400–Pantsir 'Tandem': The New-Old Feature of Russian A2/AD Capabilities," *Eurasia Daily Monitor* 15,[14] (James Town Foundation), January 30, 2018: https://jamestown.org/program/s-400-pantsir-tandem-new-old-feature-russian-a2-ad-capabilities/.

18 Federico Castanedo, "A Review of Data Fusion Techniques," *The Scientific World Journal* 2013, article ID 704504, https://www.hindawi.com/journals/tswj/2013/704504/.

19 Alket Cecaj, Marco Mamei, and Franco Zambonelli, "Re-identification and information fusion between anonymized CDR and social network data," *Journal of Ambient Intelligence and Humanized Computing* 7, no. 1, February 2016, 83–96.

20 U.S. Department of the Navy, "CEC – Cooperative Engagement Capability," *United States Navy Fact File,* updated January 25, 2017, https://www.navy.mil/navydata/fact_display.asp?cid=2100&tid=325&ct=2.

21 Joe Gould, "Electronic Warfare: What U.S. Army Can Learn From Ukraine," *Defense News,* August 2, 2015, https://www.defensenews.com/home/2015/08/02/electronic-warfare-what-us-army-can-learn-from-ukraine/.

22 Alexandr Kondratiev, Будущее сетецентрических войн ("The Future of Net-centric Wars"), *NVO,* September 7, 2012, http://nvo.ng.ru/concepts/2012-09-07/1_web_war.html.

23 Lt. Gen. Paul Van Riper (interview), "The Immutable Nature of War," *Nova,* PBS, May 3, 2004.

24 Makarenko Sergei, Подавление Сетецентрических Систем Управления Радиоэлектронными Информационно Техническими Воздействиями ("Suppression of Net-centric Control Systems by Radio-electronic Informational-Technical Means"), *Control, Communications and Security Systems* 4 (2017), 26–27, https://cyberleninka.ru/article/v/podavlenie-setetsentricheskih-sistem-upravleniya-radioelektronnymi-informatsionno-tehnicheskimi-vozdeystviyami.

25 Micah Zenko, "Millennium Challenge: The Real Story of a Corrupted Military Exercise and its Legacy," *War on the Rocks,* November 5, 2015, https://warontherocks.com/2015/11/millennium-challenge-the-real-story-of-a-corrupted-military-exercise-and-its-legacy/.

26 Adm. Jay L. Johnson, Address at AFCEA WEST, San Diego, Calif., USN, CNO, January 21, 1998.

27 "Mineral-ME" (Shipborne multifunctional radar system), Naval Systems, *Rosoboronexport Catalog,* http://roe.ru/eng/catalog/naval-systems/shipborne-electronic-systems/mineral-me/.

28 Norman Friedman, *Network-Centric Warfare How Navies Learned to Fight Smarter Through Three World Wars* (Annapolis, Maryland: Naval Institute Press, 2009), photograph section (see Mineral).

29 X-41 (3M-80) Москит, http://www.airwar.ru/weapon/pkr/moskit.html.

Chapter 5

1 A review of even non-augmented Salvo Equations with hypersonic antishipping missiles of *3M22 Zircon* or *Kinzhal* classes makes that clear.

2 A going and reasonable assumption today in regard to the latest anti-shipping hypersonic weapons is that the probability of intercept of such weapons, capable of Mach=9+, well in excess of any existing anti-missile weapons, even without maneuvering on terminal approach, is statistically insignificant. That is, in a basic Salvo Model for the losses of attacked force:

$$\Delta B = \frac{\alpha A - b_3 B}{b_1}$$

where b_1 is staying power of ships in enemy force B, which is the number of the missiles required to take out of action those respective ships. It takes a single missile of such a class to put any large combatant, with the possible exception of a nuclear aircraft carrier, completely out of action, thus making $b_1 = 1$. Coefficient b_3 denotes a defensive power of the ships in B, which is the number of good enemy shots which will be destroyed or deflected by the defender—there is really no objective evidence of modern AD systems being capable of intercepting hypersonic missiles. This makes $b_3 = 0$ and, consequently, makes the multiple of $b_3 B = 0$; this is a definition of a turkey shoot, in which the attrition ΔB of the opposing force, depends strictly on a number of hypersonic missiles in A's salvo at B. In other words, the equation is reduced to:

$$\Delta B = \frac{\alpha A}{b_1} = \alpha A$$

because $b_1 = 1$ Alpha (α) denotes the striking power of A, which is the number of missiles which would hit the target if there were no defense. There is no defense currently and this effectively eliminates B as a player in case of a missile exchange with A, thus making the exchange mostly a matter of reliability of missiles themselves.

3 U.S. Government Accountability Office, *National Security: Long-Range Emerging Threats Facing the United States as Identified by Federal Agencies,* report to Congressional Committees, December 13, 2018, 4.

4 Ben Brimelow, "China and Russia are 'aggressively pursuing' hypersonic weapons—and the U.S. doesn't have any defenses," *Business Insider,* March 20, 2018.

5 В Минобороны сообщили об успешных испытаниях ракеты «Кинжал» в сложных метеоусловиях ("Ministry of Defense reported successful tests of Kinzhal missile under adverse weather conditions"), *TASS Russian News Agency,* February 20, 2019, https://tass.ru/armiya-i-opk/6139382.

6 "Kalibr and Onyx cruise missiles engage terrorists' objects in Syria," Russian Defense Ministry video release, *YouTube,* November 15, 2016, https://youtu.be/6S6UuH9OnDg.

7 Sydney J. Freedberg, "Anti-Aircraft Missile Sinks Ship: Navy SM-6," *Breaking Defense,* March 7, 2016.

8 Эксперт: «Цирконы» нейтрализуют систему управления ракетами США в Европе за пять минут ("Expert: Zircons will neutralize the American system of missile control in Europe in 5 minutes"), *TASS Russian News Agency,* February 20, 2019, https://tass.ru/armiya-i-opk/6141953.

9 Charlie Gao, "Russia's Zicron Hypersonic Missile: Now in Land-Attack Mode?" *The National Interest,* March 9, 2019.

10 Dmitry Drobnitsky, Звёздные войны. Эпизод второй ("Star Wars, Episode Two"), *Russian RT,* January 18, 2019, https://russian.rt.com/opinion/594084-drobnickii-zvyozdnye-voiny-ssha-rossiya.

11 На "Севмаше" заложили последний "Ясень" ("The Last Yasen was laid down at Sevmash"), *Flotprom,* July 28, 2017, https://flotprom.ru/2017/Севмаш16/.

12 "Some Details on Russian Navy Latest Submarine: The Project 885M Yasen-M K-561 Kazan," *Navy Recognition Guide,* April 25, 2017, http://www.navyrecognition.com/index.php/news/defence-news/2017/april-2017-navy-naval-forces-defense-industry-technology-maritime-security-global-news/5137-some-details-on-russian-navy-latest-submarine-the-project-885m-yasen-m-k-561-kazan.html.

13 Dr. Carlo Kopp, "Soviet/Russian Cruise Missiles, Technical Report APA-TR-2009-0805," *Air Power Australia,* last modified January 27, 2014, http://www.ausairpower.net/APA-Rus-Cruise-Missiles.html#mozTocId109867.

14 Alberto A. Soto, *The Flaming Datum Problem with Varying Speed,* Compiled by Naval Post Graduate School, Monterey, Calif. (Storming Media, 2000), 4.

The modelling of the expected number of detections for a random search in an expanding disk can be modelled per A. Washburn, *Search and Detection* (Institute for Operations Research and Management Sciences, 1996):

$$\int_{\tau}^{\infty} \frac{2RV}{\pi y(t)^2} \, dt$$

where V is the searcher's (helicopter) speed, R is the range of its cookie cutter sensor, τ is the delay of the helicopter arriving at the datum and *y(t)* is the expanding disk radius at time *t*.

15 Источник: ракету "Циркон" примут на вооружение ВМФ в 2023 году ("Source: Zircon Missile will be Accepted for Service by Navy in 2023") *TASS Russian News Agency,* March 20, 2019, https://tass.ru/armiya-i-opk/6237846.

16 "Yakhont," *Deagel.com*, http://www.deagel.com/Offensive-Weapons/Yakhont_a001021001.aspx.

17 Russian Ministry of Defense, "Russian Subs vs. Terrorists: 10 cruise missiles hit targets in Syria," *RT,* October 5, 2017, https://youtu.be/xTn94lhVulY.

18 Dr. Mark B. Schneider, "The Renewed Backfire Bomber Threat to the U.S. Navy," USNI *Proceedings* 145/1/1,391 (January 2019), https://www.usni.org/magazines/proceedings/2019/january/renewed-backfire-bomber-threat-us-navy.

19 "Russia's upgraded strategic bomber to get hypersonic missiles," *TASS Russian News Agency,* August 16, 2018, http://tass.com/defense/1017461.

20 Schneider, "The Renewed Backfire Bomber Threat," *supra* note 18.

21 Richard Pipes, "Why the Soviet Union Thinks it Could Fight and Win a Nuclear War," in Douglas J. Murray and Paul R. Viotti (Eds.), *The Defense Policies of Nations: Comparative Study* (Baltimore, Maryland: The John Hopkins University Press, 1982), 135.

22 Steven Donald Smith, "Pentagon Hot Dog Stand: Cold War Legend, to be Torn Down," American Forces Press Service, September 20, 2006, http://archive.defense.gov/news/newsarticle.aspx?id=1049.

23 James Slagle, "New Russian Military Doctrine: Sign of the Times," *Parameters,* Spring 1994, 94.
Slagle quotes the 1992 presentation of then Chief of Strategy Faculty of Russia's Academy of General Staff Lieutenant-General Klokotov:

> "I would like to emphasize here that the Persian Gulf war was taken as the standard in studying the strategic nature of possible war. It would appear that this position, adopted in the draft 'Fundamentals of Russian Military Doctrine,' is dangerous. The fact is that this war [was] 'strange' in all respects [and] cannot serve as a standard."

24 Holger Nehring and Megan Dee, "We war-gamed an escalation of the Ukraine-Russia crisis—here's what it taught us about the real world," *The Conversation,* March 20, 2019, https://theconversation.com/we-war-gamed-an-escalation-of-the-ukraine-russia-crisis-heres-what-it-taught-us-about-the-real-world-113802.

25 "Transcript: President Obama Iraq speech," *BBC News,* December 15, 2011, http://www.bbc.com/news/world-us-canada-16191394.

26 В России на всех стратегических направлениях созданы группировки носителей крылатых ракет ("The groupings of carriers of cruise missiles have been deployed at all strategic directions in Russia"), *TASS Russian News Agency,* March 24, 2018, https://tass.ru/armiya-i-opk/5062476.

27 "Tests of Burevestnik nuclear powered cruise missile successfully completed, says source," *TASS Russian News Agency,* February 16, 2019, http://tass.com/defense/1045012.

28 Amanda Macias, "Vladimir Putin's so-called missile with unlimited range is too expensive for the Kremlin—and has yet to fly farther than 22 miles," *CNBC,* March 22, 2019, https://www.cnbc.com/2019/03/22/putins-missile-with-unlimited-range-is-too-expensive-and-hasnt-flown-more-than-22-miles.html.

29 "KRND Burevestnik [Petrel] SSC-X-9 Skyfall," Weapons of Mass Destruction (WMD), *GlobalSecurity.org*, https://www.globalsecurity.org/wmd/world/russia/krnd.htm.

Global Security cites Igor Korotchenko:

> "Igor Korotchenko, editor-in-chief of the *National Defense* magazine, in his turn, called the message of the American channel a purposeful information operation of the United States. According to him, it is timed to the opened forum 'Army-2018' in order to discredit the new Russian developments, to sow doubts about them. According to the interlocutor of the agency, there is a high probability that behind the message of the American television channel are the structures of the Pentagon, which are responsible for information operations in cyberspace."

30 Sydney J. Freedberg Jr., "Lasers: Beyond the Power Problem," *Breaking Defense,* March 25, 2019, https://breakingdefense.com/2019/03/lasers-beyond-the-power-problem/.

Chapter 6

1 "Aircraft losses during the Vietnam War" from *USAF Operations Report,* November 30, 1973, in John M. Campbell and Michael Hill, *Roll Call: Thud: A Photographic Record of the Republic F-105 Thunderchief* (Atglen, Pa.: Schiffer Publishing Ltd.), 1996. Chris Hobson, "Vietnam Air Losses, USAF, USN, USMC," *Fixed-Wing Aircraft Losses in Southeast Asia 1961–1973* (North Branch, Minn.: Specialty Press, 2001), https://vietnamwar-database.blogspot.com/2010/11/aircraft-losses-during-vietnam-war.html.

2 Richard P. Hallion and Adam Tooby, *Rolling Thunder 1965–68: Johnson's air war over Vietnam* (Osprey Publishing, February 22, 2018), 178.

3 Abraham Rabinovich, "The air force's lost chances to turn around the Yom Kippur War," *Jerusalem Post,* September 30, 2017, https://www.jpost.com/International/The-air-forces-last-chances-to-turn-around-the-Yom-Kippur-War-506253.

4 Sam LaGrone, "Pentagon Drops Air Sea Battle Name, Concept Lives On," *USNI News,* January 20, 2015, https://news.usni.org/2015/01/20/pentagon-drops-air-sea-battle-name-concept-lives.

5 Ibid.

6 U.S. Department of Defense, Air Sea Battle Office, Department of Defense, *Air-Sea Battle: Services Collaboration to Address Anti-Access and Area Denial Challenges (*March 2013), 4.

7 Peter Baumont and Andrew Roth, "Russia claims Syria air defenses shot down 71 of 103 missiles," *The Guardian,* April 14, 2018, https://www.theguardian.com/world/2018/apr/14/russia-claims-syria-air-defences-shot-down-majority-missiles.

8 "Trump's Big Flop In Syria," *Publius Tacitus,* April 15, 2018, http:// turcopolier.typepad.com/sic_semper_tyrannis/2018/04/trumps-big-flop-in-syria-by-publius-tacitus.html#more.

9 "China successfully tests Russia's S-400 missile air defense," *Times of India,* December 27, 2018, https://timesofindia.indiatimes.com/world/china/china-successfully-tests-russias-s-400-missile-air-defence-system/articleshow/67267423.cms.

10 Vikas Pandey, "S-400: India missile defense purchase in U.S.-Russia crosshairs," *BBC News,* October 5, 2018, https://www.bbc.com/news/world-asia-india-45757556.

11 "U.S. warns Turkey not to buy Russian S-400 missile system," *Al Jazeera,* March 5, 2019, https://www.aljazeera.com/news/2019/03/warns-turkey-buy-russian-400-missile-system-190306043845582.html.

12 Mike Stone and Humeyra Pamuk, "U.S. halts F-35 equipment to Turkey, protests its plans to buy from Russia," *Reuters,* April 1, 2019, https://news.yahoo.com/exclusive-u-sends-message-turkey-halts-f-35-184055464--finance.html.

13 Michael Peck, "F-35 Failure? Did a Russian-Made Missile Really Hit an Israeli F-35 Fighter?" *The National Interest,* December 12, 2018, https://nationalinterest.org/blog/buzz/f-35-failure-did-russian-made-missile-really-hit-israeli-f-35-fighter-38512.

14 David Ochmanek, Peter A. Wilson, Brenna Allen, John Speed Meyers, and Carter C. Price, "U.S. Military Capabilities and Forces for

a Dangerous World," *Rethinking the U.S. Approach to Force Planning,* (RAND Corporation, 2017), 87.

15 Ibid., 98, Table 7.1.

16 "The U.S. military 'gets its ass handed to it' in World War 3 simulation—researchers," *RT,* March 11, 2019, https://www.rt.com/usa/453550-us-loses-world-war-three/.

17 Amanda Macias, "Russia quietly conducted the world's longest surface-to-air missile test," *CNBC,* May 24, 2018, https://www.cnbc.com/2018/05/24/russia-quietly-conducted-the-worlds-longest-surface-to-air-missile-test.html.

18 "E-3 AWACS (Sentry) Airborne Warning and Control System," *Air Force Technology,* https://www.airforce-technology.com/projects/e3awacs/.

19 "Russia's latest S-500, S-350 systems to enter service soon," *TASS Russian News Agency,* March 1, 2019, http://tass.com/defense/1046997.

20 Captain George Galdorisi, U.S. Navy (Retired), "Unleash Directed-Energy Weapons," USNI *Proceedings,* 145/4/1,394 (April 2019), https://www.usni.org/magazines/proceedings/2019/april/unleash-directed-energy-weapons.

21 Barry D. Watts, *The Foundations of U.S. Air Doctrine: The Problem of Friction in War* (Maxwell Air Force Base, Ala.: Air University Press, December 1984), 1.

22 John Hillen, Robert Pape, and Earl Tilford, Jr., "Can Air Power Alone Win a War? *Slate,* April 14, 1999, https://slate.com/news-and-politics/1999/04/can-air-power-alone-win-a-war.html.

23 George S. Patton, Jr., *War as I knew It: The Battle Memoirs of "Blood 'N Guts",* Reissue edition (Boston: Houghton Mifflin, 1995), Introduction by Rick Atkinson, xv–xvi.

24 Greg Kopchuk, "Allied Air Power Was Decisive Factor in Western Europe," *Armchair General,* September 22, 2009, http://armchairgeneral.com/allied-air-power-was-decisive-factor-in-western-europe.htm.

25 Andrei Martyanov, *Losing Military Supremacy: The Myopia of American Strategic Planning* (Atlanta: Clarity Press, Inc., 2018), 79–80.

26 Robert Farley, "Could Air Power Have Won the Vietnam War?" *The National Interest,* September 13, 2014, https://nationalinterest.org/

feature/could-airpower-have-won-the-vietnam-war-11270.

27 Joseph A. Gattuso, Jr., and Lori J. Tanner, "Set and Drift: Naval Force in the New Century," *Naval War College Review,* January 1, 2001.

28 Sanjeev Miglani and Krishna N. Das, "Modi hails India as military space power after anti-satellite missile test," *Reuters,* March 27, 2019.

29 "Russian S-300 anti-missiles finally deployed in Iran," *RT,* May 10, 2016, https://www.rt.com/news/342483-s-300-deployed-iran/.

30 Patrick Tucker, "Amid NATO Infighting, the Future of the F-35 Is Shrinking," *Defense One,* June 19, 2018, https://www.defenseone.com/technology/2018/06/ thanks-nato-infighting-future-f-35-shrinking/149136/.

31 Andrew Korybko, "Egypt's $2 Billion Su-35 Deal Will Secure the Sinai and Offshore Gas Reserves," *Oriental Review,* February 23, 2019, https://orientalreview.org/2019/03/23/egypts-2-billion-su-35-deal-will-secure-the-sinai-and-offshore-gas-reserves/.

32 Shaul Shay, "Report: Egypt, Russia Sign $2B Deal for Su-35 Fighter Jets," *Israel Defense,* March 19, 2019, https://www.israeldefense.co.il/en/node/37858.

Chapter 7

1 Saudi Arabia Military Strength 2019, *Global Fire Power Rankings,* https://www.globalfirepower.com/country-military-strength-detail.asp?country_id=saudi-arabia.

2 Declan Walsh, "The Tragedy of Saudi Arabia Wars, *New York Times,* October 26, 2018, https://www.nytimes.com/ interactive/2018/10/26/world/middleeast/saudi-arabia-war-yemen.html.

3 Boris Lifshitz, Первый выстрел Наполеона по России был сделан фальшивыми деньгами ("The First Shot at Russia by Napoleon Was Made by Counterfeit Money"), *MK,* December 13, 2016, https://www.mk.ru/economics/700let/2016/12/10/pervyy-vystrel-napoleona-po-rossii-byl-sdelan-falshivymi-dengami.html.

4 Patrick Lang, "Will Saudi Arabia Survive the Yemen War?" *Sic Semper Tyranis,* September 25, 2015, https://turcopolier.typepad.com/ sic_semper_tyrannis/2015/09/will-saudi-arabia-survive-the-yemen-war-first-published-.html.

5 "2019 Military Strength Ranking," *Global Fire Power,* https://www.globalfirepower.com/countries-listing.asp.

6 Saudi Arabia 2017 Gross Domestic Product Based on Purchasing-Power-Parity (PPP) Valuation of Country GDP, *International Monetary Fund World Economic Outlook Database, 2017.* For Iran PPP, GDP value is taken from CIA, *The World Fact Book.*

7 Sergei Mikheev, Честной торговли не бывает, экономическая наука – враньё ("There is no fair trade, economic science is a lie"), *Iron Logic, YouTube,* April 9, 2019, https://youtu.be/JeOyzq97jC8.

8 "Iran Profile," *MIT Atlas,* https://atlas.media.mit.edu/en/profile/country/irn/.

9 "2019 Military Strength Ranking" *supra* note 5.

10 "Wilkerson: We can bomb Iran for 70 days around the clock," *RT,* March 18, 2010, https://youtu.be/gzvP5p2SMec.

11 Charles P. Blair, "War with Iran? Revisiting the Potentially Staggering Costs to the Global Economy," *FAS,* March 23, 2013, https://fas.org/blogs/security/2013/05/war-with-iran-revisiting-the-potentially-staggering-costs-to-the-global-economy/.

12 Ibid.

13 Zachary Keck, "Exposed: Iran's Super Strategy to Crush America in a War," *The National Interest,* June 20, 2015, https://nationalinterest.org/feature/exposed-irans-super-strategy-crush-america-war-13152.

14 Hezbollah received Chinese C-802–subsonic ASMs, one of then hit INS Hanit in 2006. Amos Harel, "Soldier killed, 3 missing after Navy vessel hit off Beirut coast," *Haaretz.com,* July 16, 2006, https://web.archive.org/web/20060718032259/http://haaretz.com/hasen/spages/738695.html.

15 "World's 'Deadliest' Missile BrahMos to Achieve Hypersonic Speed Within 7 Years," *Sputnik News,* July 12, 2017.

16 Robert Haddick, "China's Most Dangerous Missile (So Far)," *War on the Rocks,* July 2, 2014, https://warontherocks.com/2014/07/chinas-most-dangerous-missile-so-far/.

17 Alexei Ramm and Bogdan Stepovoy, Компактный гиперзвук: ВМФ получит облегченные ракеты «Циркон» ("Compact Hyper-Sound: Navy will receive lightweight Zircon missiles"), *Izvestia,* January 22, 2019, https://iz.ru/833837/aleksei-ramm-bogdan-stepovoi/kompaktnyi-giperzvuk-vmf-poluchit-oblegchennye-rakety-tcirkon.

18 Jamie Seidel, "'Sink two aircraft carriers': Chinese Admiral's chilling recipe to dominate the South China Sea," *News Corp Australia Network,* January 2, 2019, https://www.news.com.au/ technology/innovation/military/sink-two-aircraft-carriers-chinese-admirals-chilling-recipie-to-dominate-the-south-china-sea/news-story/ aaa8c33d57da62e7d5e28e791aa26e0f.

19 James Holmes, "Yes, China Could Sink a U.S. Navy Aircraft Carrier, But Don't Bet On It," *The National Interest,* January 11, 2019, https://nationalinterest.org/blog/buzz/yes-china-could-sink-us-navy-aircraft-carrier-don%E2%80%99t-bet-it-41227?page=0%2C1.

20 When Republicans Rejected John Bolton. Antony J. Blinken. New York Times. March 23, 2018, https://www.nytimes.com/2018/03/23/ opinion/john-bolton-republicans.html.

21 Julian Barnes and Adam Goldman, "Gina Haspel Relies on Spy Skills to Connect With Trump; He Doesn't Always Listen," *New York Times,* April 16, 2019, https://www.nytimes.com/2019/04/16/us/ politics/gina-haspel-trump.html.

22 "BREAKING! Putin On Mueller Report: It's Total Nonsense—A Mountain Gave Birth To A Mouse!" *Russia Insight, YouTube,* April 9, 2019, https://youtu.be/q43_fS8rnfw.

23 "Russia's Lavrov snubs U.S. journalist: 'Whatever I answer, you'll write what you want,'" *ProductiehuisEU, YouTube,* February 16, 2019, https://youtu.be/ltEgMF9S0QI.

24 Ron Ridenour, *The Russian Peace Threat: Pentagon on Alert* (New York: Punto Press Publishing, 2018), 400.

Conclusion

1 Philip M. Giraldi, "Rumors of War: Washington is Looking for a Fight," *Strategic Culture Foundation,* April 18, 2019, https://www. strategic-culture.org/news/2019/04/18/rumors-war-washington-is-looking-for-fight.html.

2 Julie Ray, "Gallup's Top World Findings for 2018," *Gallup,* December 26, 2018, https://news.gallup.com/poll/245561/gallup-top-world-findings-2018.aspx.

3 "Happy New Year? The world's getting slowly more cheerful," *BBC News,* December 30, 2013, https://www.bbc.com/news/ world-25496299.

4 Giraldi, "Rumors of War."

5 Vladimir Ilyich Lenin, "Imperialism as a special stage of capitalism" (Chapter VII), *Imperialism, the Highest Stage of Capitalism: A Popular Outline,* Marxists.org, https://www.marxists.org/archive/lenin/works/1916/imp-hsc/ch07.htm.

6 Michael Collins, "The Financialization of the Economy Hurts Manufacturing," *Industry Week,* September 25, 2015, https://www.industryweek.com/competitiveness/financialization-economy-hurts-manufacturing.

7 Shannon Selin, "10 Things Napoleon Never Said," *Imagining the Bounds of History Blog,* July 10, 2014, https://shannonselin.com/2014/07/10-things-napoleon-never-said/.

8 Lidia Misnik, Гроза Европы: в Калининграде развернули «Мурманск-БН» ("Menace to Europe: 'Murmansk BN' has been deployed to Kaliningrad"), *Gazeta.Ru,* April 26, 2019, https://www.gazeta.ru/army/2019/04/26/12323509.shtml.

9 Brookings Institute, Discussion on Nuclear Deterrence, *CSPAN,* April 25, 2019, 2:13am-4:14am EDT.

10 Julian E. Barnes and Adam Goldman, "Gina Haspel Relies on Spy Skills to Connect with Trump. He Doesn't Always Listen.," *New York Times,* April 16, 2019.

11 Natalya Dembinskaya, Это конец: под мировую экономику заложили бомбу на 243 триллиона долларов ("This Is the End: The 243 Trillion Dollar Bomb Was Placed under the Global Economy"), *Ria.Ru,* April 26, 2019, https://ria.ru/20190429/1553097220.html.

12 Ibid.

13 Colonel Lawrence Wilkerson, Keynote, Massachusetts Peace Action 2019, *YouTube,* March 10, 2019, https://youtu.be/tYPHcLa9YAc

14 James Howard Kunstler, "Tom Petty was Right," *Clusterfuck Nation* (blog), April 29, 2019, https://kunstler.com/clusterfuck-nation/tom-petty-was-right/.

15 Gilbert Doctorow, "Vladimir Putin to the West: 'We Will Bury You!'" *Antiwar.com,* February 2, 2019, https://original.antiwar.com/gilbert_doctorow/2019/02/01/vladimir-putin-to-the-west-we-will-bury-you/.

16 Dexter Filkins, "John Bolton on the Warpath," *New Yorker,* April 29, 2019.

17 Ibid.

18 Ibid.

19 Daniel Larison, "The Fanatic Running Trump's Foreign Policy," *The American Conservative,* April 29, 2019, https://www.theamericanconservative.com/larison/the-fanatic-running-trumps-foreign-policy/.

20 Stephen M. Walt, "America Isn't as Powerful as It Thinks It Is," *Foreign Policy,* April 26, 2019, https://foreignpolicy.com/2019/04/26/america-isnt-as-powerful-as-it-thinks-it-is/.

21 Nicholas Sakelaris, "Putin threatens to target U.S. 'decision-making centers' if missiles deployed," *UPI,* February 20, 2019, https://www.upi.com/Putin-threatens-to-target-U.S.-decision-making-centers-if-missiles-deployed/2101550662756/.

22 Paul Craig Roberts, "Venezuela Is An Opportunity for Russia and China to Change the World," *Unz Review,* February 8, 2019.

23 Robert W. Merry, "America, We Have a Problem," *The American Conservative,* April 30, 2019.

24 Andrei Raevsky (The Saker), "The End of the 'Wars on the Cheap' for the United States," *The Unz Review,* August 4, 2017, http://www.unz.com/tsaker/the-end-of-the-wars-on-the-cheap-for-the-united-states/.

25 Andrei Martyanov, *Losing Military Supremacy: The Myopia of American Strategic Planning* (Atlanta: Clarity Press, Inc., 2018), 224.

26 Alexandr Tvardovsky, *Vasily Tyorkin,* https://web.archive.org/web/20030713041544/http://www.litera.ru/stixiya/authors/tvardovskij/pereprava-pereprava-bereg.html.

Postscript

1 "'Laser weapons' to define Russia's military potential in 21st century—Putin," *RT,* May 17, 2019, https://www.rt.com/russia/459586-putin-laser-weapons-remarks/.

2 Lucy Draper, "The Wedding That Became a Funeral: U.S. Still Silent One Year On from Deadly Yemen Drone Strike," *Newsweek,* December 12, 2014, https://www.newsweek.com/wedding-became-funeral-us-still-silent-one-year-deadly-yemen-drone-strike-291403.

3 "VFW Wants New Medal Ranking Lowered. VFW believes Distinguished Warfare Medal should not outrank the Bronze Star, Purple Heart," *VFW,* February 14, 2013, https://www.

vfw.org/media-and-events/latest-releases/archives/2013/2/
vfw-wants-new-medal-ranking-lowered.

4 Andrei Epifantsev, Сравнение прогнозов П. Фельгенгауэра
с действительностью в конфликте с Грузией ("Comparison of
forecasts by P. Falgenhauer with reality of the conflict with Georgia"),
War and Peace, December 09, 2009, http://www.warandpeace.ru/ru/
exclusive/view/39201/.

5 John Mearsheimer, *The Tragedy of Great Power Politics,* updated
ed. (New York: W.W. Norton & Company, 2003), Preface.

6 Sergei Gorshkov, *The Sea Power of the State* (Oxford, U.K.:
Pergamon Press, Ltd., 1979), 253–254.

7 Norman Polmar and Jurrien S. Noot, *Submarines of the Russian
and Soviet Navies, 1718–1990* (Annapolis: Naval Institute Press, 1991),
210.

8 Jerry Hendrix and Harry Foster, "China has Impressive A2/AD
Capabilities, but Smart Positioning Can Let the Navy Avoid Them,"
The National Interest, November 10, 2018.

9 Alexander Shishkin, Реальные боевые возможности гигантского
флота Китая явно преувеличены ("Real Combat Capabilities of
Gigantic Chinese Navy are Obviously Exaggerated"), *Vzglyad,* July 13,
2018, https://vz.ru/world/2018/7/13/932028.html.

10 Congressional Research Service, *China's Actions in South and
East China Seas: Implications for U.S. Interests—Background and
Issues for Congress,* Ronald O'Rourke, August 1, 2018, 49.

11 Nengye Liu, "China-Russia Trouble on the Arctic Silk Road?"
The Diplomat, July 21, 2017.

12 Ryan Pickrell, "China has a New Hypersonic Anti-Ship
Missile that It Claims Could Destroy a U.S. Warship in One Hit,"
Task and Purpose, November 8, 2018, https://taskandpurpose.com/
china-hypersonic-anti-ship-missile.

13 "Russia must have hypersonic defense before others get such
weapon systems—Putin," *RT,* May 14, 2019, https://www.rt.com/
news/459247-putin-hypersonic-defense-sooner/.

14 U.S. Department of Defense, Office of the Under Secretary of
Defense, *Defense Budget Overview: United States Department of
Defense Fiscal Year 2020 Budget Request,* March, 2019, 1–9.

15 "The United States declared ICBM 'Sarmat' and complex

'Avangard' under the start-3," *WeapoNews,* May 16, 2019, https://weaponews.com/news/65350721-the-united-states-declared-icbm-sarmat-and-complex-avangard-under-the-.html.

16 Alan Chanter, "80 cm Gustav Railway Gun," *World War II Database,* https://ww2db.com/weapon.php?q=89.

17 Путин заявил, что до 2028 года будет закуплено 76 самолетов Су-57 ("Putin announced that 76 SU-57 will be purchased before 2028"), *TASS Russian News Agency,* May 15, 2019, https://tass.ru/armiya-i-opk/6434341.

18 Dave Majumdar, "Russia's Next Fighter Could Come Loaded with Stealth Killing Radar and Lasers," *The National Interest,* August 1, 2017, https://nationalinterest.org/blog/the-buzz/russias-next-fighter-could-come-loaded-stealth-killing-radar-21748.

19 Peace Action Maine, "Maine 2019 Spring Gathering & Colonel Lawrence Wilkerson Speech," *Portland Media Center, YouTube,* May 7, 2019, https://youtu.be/kZA2yIFkhKg.

INDEX

Made in the USA
Coppell, TX
20 May 2021

56011958R00134